P9-CLC-001

AN UNAUTHORIZED BIOGRAPHY BY LEXI RYALS

BEST FRIENDS FOREVER
SELENA GOMEZ
& DEMI LOVATO

PRICE STERN SLOAN
Published by the Penguin Group
Penguin Group (USA) Inc., 375 Hudson Street, New York, New York 10014, USA
Penguin Group (Canada), 90 Eglinton Avenue East, Suite 700,
Toronto, Ontario M4P 2Y3, Canada
(a division of Pearson Penguin Canada Inc.)
Penguin Books Ltd., 80 Strand, London WC2R 0RL, England
Penguin Group Ireland, 25 St. Stephen's Green, Dublin 2, Ireland
(a division of Penguin Books Ltd.)
Penguin Group (Australia), 250 Camberwell Road, Camberwell, Victoria 3124, Australia
(a division of Pearson Australia Group Pty. Ltd.)
Penguin Books India Pvt. Ltd., 11 Community Centre, Panchsheel Park,
New Delhi—110 017, India
Penguin Group (NZ), 67 Apollo Drive, Rosedale, North Shore 0632, New Zealand
(a division of Pearson New Zealand Ltd.)
Penguin Books (South Africa) (Pty.) Ltd., 24 Sturdee Avenue,
Rosebank, Johannesburg 2196, South Africa

Penguin Books Ltd., Registered Offices:
80 Strand, London WC2R 0RL, England

Photo credits: Cover: courtesy of Chris Hatcher/PR Photos; Insert photos: first page courtesy
of Jean-Paul Aussenard/WireImage; second page courtesy of Andrew H. Walker/Getty Images;
third page courtesy of Mark Sullivan/WireImage for Elizabeth Glaser Pediatric AIDS, Gregg
DeGuire/WireImage; fourth page courtesy of Jason Merritt/FilmMagic; fifth page courtesy of
Dimitrios Kambouris/WireImage, Gregg DeGuire/WireImage; sixth page courtesy of Steve Granitz/
WireImage; seventh page courtesy of Chris Hatcher/PR Photos, Jason Merritt/FilmMagic; eighth
page courtesy of Dimitrios Kambouris/WireImage

Library of Congress Control Number: 2008024920

ISBN 978-0-8431-3366-0   10 9 8 7 6 5 4 3 2 1

AN UNAUTHORIZED BIOGRAPHY BY LEXI RYALS

BEST FRIENDS FOREVER
SELENA GOMEZ
& DEMI LOVATO

TABLE OF CONTENTS

INTRODUCTION

One hot, sticky summer day in Las Colinas, Texas, in 1999, a line of over 1,400 kids and their parents snaked around the parking lot of The Studios, where one of the most popular children's shows of all time was filmed. That show was *Barney & Friends,* and it was, and still is, a smash hit with both kids and parents. The educational show stars a large, friendly purple dinosaur who sings, dances, and teaches elementary-school kids about manners, basic skills like reading and counting, and life lessons about things like safety.

The children waiting in line were there for an open audition to be series regulars on *Barney.* Most of them had no acting experience, but they all desperately wanted to be on the show. The kids ranged in age from five to ten years old, were of different races, and had drastically different looks. But the one thing they had in common was that they were all very talented. Everyone knew that the competition would be stiff, but they were willing to wait anyway, just for a shot at impressing the casting agents.

Somewhere toward the middle of the line, two little girls stood next to each other. One was a pretty seven-year-old of Hispanic descent named Selena Gomez. She had long black hair, olive skin, and big chocolate-brown eyes. The other was Demi Lovato, a six-year-old with long, light-brown hair and bangs, round glasses, and a toothy smile. The two girls smiled shyly at each other as they stood next to their mothers and watched the line slowly creep forward. They were both very nervous and neither of them was that excited about the long wait. They stood in silence for a while, each of them wondering exactly what they would have to do during the audition.

Finally, Demi decided she might as well have some fun while she waited. She spread her jacket out on the ground where they were standing and took out some crayons and a coloring book. Then she turned to Selena and asked her very politely if she would like to color with her. Selena happily said yes and the two girls sat down and began coloring together. They chatted about school, their moms, and their friends, and soon they were giggling as if they'd been friends forever. By the time Selena and Demi made it to the front of the line, they didn't want to stop hanging out. But they had to go in for the auditions, so they wished each other luck and both went in separately to try out.

Luckily for Selena and Demi, they nailed the auditions and the subsequent callbacks and were hired for the show. They filmed together until the end of fifth grade, and they became best friends over that time. They helped each other through fights with other friends, boy trouble, and the disappointments of bad auditions and failed pilots. They also celebrated together when they made good grades, met cute boys, nailed auditions, and landed amazing roles. When Demi and Selena first met, they had no idea how successful they would be in the future, and they certainly never imagined that they would be big Disney Channel stars just a few years later.

Selena Gomez and Demi Lovato are two of the most talented and dynamic teen stars out there, but what really makes them stand out are their down-to-earth attitudes. These two are as fresh, genuine, and funny as they were the day they arrived in Hollywood from Texas, and they owe that, in large part, to their incredible friendship. They help keep each other from getting carried away in the fast-paced entertainment world and they always have each other's backs. That was true when they were seven years old singing on *Barney & Friends* and it will be just as true in the future, no matter what it holds. And considering just how talented Selena and Demi are, they will probably be celebrating their successes together for many years to come!

CHAPTER 1
TEXAS GIRLS

They say everything is bigger in Texas, so it's no surprise that two larger-than-life stars like Selena Gomez and Demi Lovato both grew up there. Texas is well known for its big-haired beauty queens, delicious Tex-Mex food, and famous landmarks like the Alamo. There are some pretty big cities in Texas, like Houston, Dallas, San Antonio, and Austin, but most of Texas is made up of small, friendly towns. Selena Gomez grew up in a little town called Grand Prairie, b she wasn't always a southern girl. Selena was actually thousands of miles away in New York City!

On July 22, 1992, the Gomez family w baby Selena into the world in a hospital in New Selena's mother, Mandy, is of Italian descent a is of Mexican heritage, so Selena was born olive-toned skin, dark hair, and big brown ey certainly thought she was the most beau entire world. Selena's dad, in particular, j daughter had serious charisma and star power, even as a newborn. He named her Selena after the Mexican superstar singer Selena Quintanilla-Perez.

Selena Quintanilla-Perez was one of the most adored Mexican-American singers in the history of music. She specialized in a type of pop-folk music called Tejano, which is extremely popular. Selena recorded nine albums with her band, only one of which was in English. She was the first female Tejano singer to ever have a gold record and she won numerous awards in the Latin community. Selena had just ished her first crossover album in English in 1995 when was tragically murdered by her fan club president. Her ere shocked and outraged by the loss, and many of rney to Corpus Christi, Texas, every year to pay cts at her grave. Selena Gomez's father took her she was little so that she could see how many the star she was named after. Selena Gomez elena Quintanilla-Perez's music, and she's red to share her name with the star who people in her short life.

With such a superstar name, it's really no wonder that Selena had her eyes set on performing when she was only six years old, but she was certainly helped along by the fact that she had talent in her blood. Selena's mother Mandy was a stage actress who did a lot of work in the New York City theater community. She was a whiz with stage makeup and a brilliant actress. But shortly after Selena was born, the family packed up and moved down to Texas, where Selena's parents were both from. Selena loved Texas and she settled into life there very quickly. She grew into a precocious tomboy who loved playing outside with the boys in her neighborhood. She adored sports and was curious about everything around her. She was also incredibly smart and determined, and her parents quickly learned not to try to force Selena to do anything she didn't want to do.

Unfortunately, when she was still little, Selena's parents got a divorce. Selena lived with Mandy, and while she definitely missed her father, she wanted both of her parents to be happy—even if it meant they weren't together. Plus, Selena had her grandparents, aunts, uncles, and cousins nearby, so she was never without plenty of family and love. "I've had the same friends since kindergarten, so everyone is still really close. And I'm really close to all my family—my cousins, my aunts, my grandmother and grandpa," Selena told *Girls' Life Magazine*.

Mandy didn't let the divorce get her down. She worked hard, and when Selena was a teenager, Mandy opened her own production company. Selena was probably very inspired by her mother's dedication to her dreams. Mandy never gave up on theater, even when times got tough, and that taught Selena that hard work really does pay off and that you always have to believe in yourself. Mandy also remarried, to a man from Michigan named Brian Teefey. Selena got along well with her stepfather and she was very excited to see her mother happy again.

While Selena was still just in elementary school, Mandy continued to work as a stage actress, which meant that Selena spent a lot of time in theaters while her mother rehearsed or performed. She probably had a lot of fun running around backstage, in the dressing rooms, and playing in the empty theaters. When Selena was about six years old, she decided that she, too, wanted to act. Selena's mom knew better than to try to stop her headstrong daughter, so she took Selena to her first audition. "My mom did a lot of theater when I was younger so I grew up around it, and I just always loved it. I loved running lines with her, and then one day I tried out for something and got it, and it all started!" Selena told PBSKids.org.

Selena was a natural entertainer. She instinctively knew when to ham it up and when to be soft, and she always impressed casting agents with her comedic timing. But Selena was very self-conscious about one thing—her looks. Most girls would kill for Selena's chocolate-brown eyes, tan skin, and thick black hair, but Selena wanted to look different when she was little. "I wanted to be like my friends. I hung out with girls who had blue eyes and blond hair and I thought, 'I want to look like them!'" Selena explained to *TWIST* magazine. But her more exotic look actually really helped Selena when she began acting, and now she couldn't be more proud of her heritage. "When

I went to auditions, I'd be in a room with a lot of blond girls, and I always stood out. It actually helped . . . that I looked different. It got me where I am today! I don't know if I would've had the opportunity to be on *Wizards of Waverly Place* if it weren't for my heritage. I realize everybody wants what they don't have. But at the end of the day, what you have inside is much more beautiful than what's on the outside!" Selena told *TWIST* magazine.

Selena was pretty set on being an actress, but she was also a pretty regular little girl. She spent plenty of time with her family and her friends from school. Selena was definitely not a girly girl, so it's no surprise that one of her best friends growing up was a boy. His name is Randy Hill and they are still very close to this day, as Selena explained to *Girls' Life Magazine*, "Yeah, I knew him ever since I was 5. He's really cool, and he's nice. People think, 'Oh, yeah, she has a guy best friend.' Yeah, because I've known him my whole life. I know everything about him, and he's sweet. Yes, I have a guy and girl best friend." Selena made a lot of other good friends when she started school as well, but most of them were boys, too. "I guess I'm a guys' girl. Back in Texas, where I'm from, I just hung out with my guy friends because they're all like older brothers. I got into a lot of drama with girls. They're very, 'Oh my gosh. She said this about you.' I was like, 'Whoa, OK. Too much drama.' Guys are like, 'Whatever,' and that's how I am," Selena told *Girls' Life Magazine*.

Selena and her friends always had a lot of fun hanging out together. "We used to walk around the blocks a lot, me and my friends. We would walk around all of the neighborhoods, but other than that it's pretty normal. You can go to skate parks, or you can go to the mall or movies with your friends," Selena explained to *Girls' Life Magazine*. The boys may not have been into makeup or shopping, but they did teach Selena about sports, and basketball is her favorite. She began playing when she was young, usually just pickup games with her friends, but then joined her school team. As she told *Girls' Life Magazine*, "I'm a huge basketball fan. My favorite is the San Antonio Spurs. I used to be on a team for school, and then I got home-schooled so not anymore."

Selena is still very close with her friends and family

in Grand Prairie and she goes home to visit them as often as she possibly can. "My mom has always told me, 'Remember where you came from.' I was surrounded by the best people back home. I'll never forget that," Selena told DiscoveryGirls.com. Selena already had amazing friends, but when she was seven years old, Selena met the girl who would go on to be her best friend for years to come, Demi Lovato.

Demetria Devonne Lovato, Demi for short, was born in Dallas, Texas, on August 20, 1992—just a few months after Selena. Baby Demi was cute as a button and a very easygoing child, but there were big things in store for the cheerful baby; she just didn't know it yet! Demi grew up in a very talented household. Her mother, Dianna, had been a Dallas Cowboys cheerleader in the 1980s and had gone on to record country music. Demi's older sister, Dallas, was musically talented as well, and made it known that she wanted to be a recording artist at the tender age of four. When Demi was little, her mother took her along to all of Dallas's shows and lessons. Luckily, Demi seemed to love all of the traveling, and was perfectly happy watching her big sis perform. With such a talented mother and older sister, it's no surprise that Demi wanted to be an entertainer, too. She loved music from day one, probably because there was always music playing in the Lovato home. Demi grew into a sassy, curious child, and because she had spent a lot of time going to auditions with her sister, it wasn't a big change for Demi when she began auditioning herself.

Demi caught the performance bug when she was about five years old. She decided she'd had enough of watching Dallas take the stage—she wanted some of that spotlight for herself! Once Demi expressed an interest in performing, her mother supported her 100 percent. Dianna enrolled Demi in acting, singing, and dancing classes and Demi began competing in talent competitions across Texas. She also joined her sister in the local shows she was doing. Demi was a natural onstage and the crowds loved her. She was charming and charismatic and absolutely adorable. Dallas helped Demi perfect her stage presence and taught her tons of dance moves. One Thanksgiving, Demi and Dallas even got the opportunity to perform at halftime for the Dallas Cowboys, with country superstar LeAnn Rimes! In addition to live shows, Demi auditioned for local commercials and voice-over work for radio, and she booked several jobs.

It was nice to be part of a family of entertainers, but it wasn't always easy to be the youngest. Demi's little sister, Madison, was born when Demi was ten, but until then it was just Demi, Dallas, and their mom. Dallas had been pursuing a musical career since she was four, and the family spent a lot of time supporting Dallas's dreams. Demi was pursuing her own goals, but at the time, Dallas was the family star. Demi was very proud of her sister, and she looked up to Dallas a lot, but there were times when Demi wished she could be the center of attention. Luckily, Demi never let having such a talented sister get her down for too long. After all, it was Dallas's success that opened a lot of doors in the Texas entertainment world for Demi, and Dallas and Demi had always been very close. Dallas was always there for Demi if she needed help with a routine, support, or just someone to talk to. They kept each other entertained when they were on the road and spent lots of time playing together when they weren't working. And when baby Madison joined the family when Demi was ten and Dallas was fifteen, they welcomed her with open arms.

As the girls got older, Dallas continued to pursue her music and honed her style into a unique funk-pop blend that her fans love. Demi, on the other hand, wasn't quite as focused. She loved music and dancing, but she also wanted to try acting. So, when she was seven years old, Demi auditioned for a regular role on a children's television series that would change her life way more than she ever expected.

CHAPTER 2
I LOVE YOU, YOU LOVE ME

"I love you, you love me. We're a happy family..." From 1988 on, thousands of kids sat in front of the television every single day to watch a giant purple dinosaur named Barney sing those famous lines. Barney is the star of *Barney & Friends,* one of the most successful children's shows in history. The show was filmed near Dallas, Texas, and it was one of the few opportunities for kids in Texas to break into show business. When Demi and Selena decided to get into acting, *Barney & Friends* seemed like a great opportunity to both of them.

Barney & Friends was the first role that Selena ever tried out for, and she was a little scared going into that audition. "I was definitely nervous; I was very shy when I was younger. I remember we had to wait in this line with about 1,400 other kids and I didn't know what I was doing. But then when I got to the audition, I realized it was just running lines, just like I always did with my mom. It was scary—and those situations are still scary for me—but it was fun at the same time," Selena told PBSKids.org. Luckily, Selena's nerves didn't hold her back. She and Demi both aced the auditions and were cast on the show.

After making it through all of those auditions, Demi and Selena were both delighted when they arrived for the first day of filming and found each other there. They hung out together between takes and soon they were getting together to play and having regular sleepovers at each other's houses. Selena and Demi didn't go to the same school, but they lived close enough to each other to hang out often. The girls were practically inseparable on set, and it was very nice for both of them to have a close friend who understood their love of acting and what it meant to be a working actress at such a young age.

Selena played the role of Gianna and Demi played Angela on *Barney & Friends* until they finished fifth grade. The girls had a lot of fun on the show and they got to do some really cool stuff. Demi, with her considerable musical talents, was always selected for scenes in which the kids played musical instruments, and Selena was a favorite for funny scenes that required comedic timing and spunk. Both girls still remember a lot of the songs they performed, and sometimes, when they are feeling really goofy, they'll sing their old favorites from the show. Selena was excited every time she got to film and she really credits *Barney & Friends* with making her into the professional she is today. "I was about 6 or 7 years old when I started with that," Selena told the *OC Register*. "I actually learned a lot from that, because I didn't know anything. That was my first audition, my first anything that I'd ever done. I think that was a real blessing."

Working on *Barney* taught Demi and Selena how to memorize lines, work with multiple cameras, move in relation to other actors, and sing and dance on camera. All of those skills would come in very handy in their future performances, so it was great that they mastered them at such a young age.

It was also pretty cool to be working on such a popular show, but it certainly wasn't easy. There were definitely kids who were jealous of Demi and Selena's success. "I'd miss a couple of weeks for *Barney* and then I'd go back to school and I'd deal with some jealousy. I wouldn't talk about the show unless somebody said, 'How was your episode?' So not a lot of people were jealous—just this one group of girls who didn't like me," Selena told DiscoveryGirls.com. It was hard for Selena to deal with people being so negative about something she was so excited about. And it did hurt her feelings to have girls she thought were her friends turn their backs on her just because she was achieving her dreams. But she stuck it out, and eventually people got over being jealous. "I mean, I got made fun of because I was in *Barney*! Just know that, at the end of the day, you will be okay and you'll always have your true friends with you," Selena said to DiscoveryGirls.com. Most of Selena's friends were, and still are, very supportive of her, as she explained to DiscoveryGirls.com. ". . . They've even come out to Los Angeles to see the show . . . I did lose a couple of friends because of the whole jealousy thing. But I look at it like a sport. Some kids play soccer. Acting is my sport."

Selena's fans are definitely glad she didn't let a little bit of jealousy get in the way of her acting career, and those girls who were mean to her are probably sad that they aren't her friends now!

Demi was a little more prepared for the jealousy from her peers. Demi's older sister, Dallas, had been performing since she was little as well, and she was there to encourage Demi and help her deal with anyone who was mean to her. Dallas actually really helped both Demi and Selena. Since the friends were pretty much inseparable, Selena was over at the Lovato house a lot. Dallas was always happy to help the younger girls practice singing and dancing. And Selena and Demi always had each other to lean on. The kids at school may not have understood why acting was so important to them, but they got each other perfectly!

Barney & Friends was an amazing opportunity for both Demi and Selena, and they wouldn't trade their time on the show for anything. It taught them all about working in the industry and was a great kick-start for their careers. They've stayed friends with a lot of other kids from the show, but most importantly, they've stayed friends with each other. Meeting in line was a coincidence, but it was working together on the show that really cemented their friendship. These days, they can't imagine what life would be like without each other! Gaining a friendship that incredible really did make their time on *Barney* worthwhile. Plus, there are very few people out there who can say that they actually know Barney!

CHAPTER 3
THE DRAMATIC DUO

Demi and Selena had an amazing time working on *Barney & Friends*, but they were also interested in pursuing more challenging roles. They loved acting, and working on *Barney* had really helped them become truly poised and professional actresses. They had both been taking acting and singing classes for a long time with Cathryn Sullivan at EveryBody Fits studio in Coppell, Texas. EveryBody Fits has classes in everything from acting, music, modeling, and theater to gymnastics, tae kwon do, and dance. And Cathryn was also the mother of a child star, Disney Channel cutie Cody Linley. Cody has appeared on *Hannah Montana* in the recurring role of Jake Ryan and in a number of made-for-television movies. Demi, Selena, and Cody all took classes together when they were little and they are still good friends today. With Cathryn's help and training, both Demi's and Selena's acting and singing skills improved, and they began auditioning for new roles.

The best friends stuck with auditions in Texas. Flying to Los Angeles to audition for roles was very expensive, and there was never a guarantee that they would book the part. There were, however, a number of commercials and shows being filmed in Texas, so they had plenty of projects to try out for. Selena landed parts in a number of commercials and when she was eleven years old, she got a small part in 2003's *Spy Kids 3-D: Game Over*, the third installment in Robert Rodriguez's *Spy Kids* franchise. The *Spy Kids* trilogy follows the son and daughter of spies, who get the chance to save the world when their parents get in trouble. In *Spy Kids 3-D*, Carmen, one of the kids, gets sucked into a sinister video game and her brother has to save her. Selena played a girl at a water park alongside stars Alexa Vega, Daryl Sabara, Sylvester Stallone, Antonio Banderas, and Salma Hayek. Selena was especially proud to be a part of a film with so many incredible stars of Latin heritage. Selena really looks up to Hispanic actresses like Salma who inspire her to be proud of her own Mexican heritage. Even though Selena's part was very small, it was still a role in a feature film and she was very excited about it. Plus seeing herself in 3-D was totally cool!

After *Spy Kids*, Selena booked a role on a made-for-television movie special of the Texas television mainstay *Walker, Texas Ranger.* The film was called *Walker, Texas Ranger: Trial by Fire*, and it first aired on October 16, 2005. Selena played the part of Julie. *Texas Ranger* is a show about Cordell Walker, played by Chuck Norris, a Texas Ranger who takes the law into his own hands when dealing with criminals. The movie was a huge hit with fans and Selena was proud to be a part of such a long-running and successful show. *Walker* fans are very devoted to the show and its star, especially in Texas. So Selena had grown up watching the show and that made it even cooler for her to be in the movie.

The next project that Selena booked was a pilot for a new children's television show called *Brain Zapped*. It was produced, written, and directed by a local filmmaker named Eliud George Garcia. Selena was cast in the lead role of Emily Garcia and she recorded the show's theme song. The show focused on reading and all of the adventures that can be found inside books. In the pilot, Selena's character, Emily, and her best friend Kingston, played by Lewis Parry, hear about something strange going on at their library. Both kids love books, so they decide to investigate. Things seem normal when they arrive, but then they see holograms popping out of books and mysterious glowing bookshelves. Soon, the two friends are sucked into one of the bookshelves and are off on a series of adventures. Most of the episode was shot on a green screen with just Selena and Lewis. Working in front of a green screen was a cool new experience for Selena. It meant that she and her costar did all of their acting while standing in a special all-green room. Then during the editing process, the editor would take all of the green out of the scene and replace it with any pre-shot background that he liked. The green screen made it easy for the director to add special effects and to make it *seem* like Selena had to journey back to prehistoric times with dinosaurs or to the North Pole. But in reality, Selena never had to leave Texas at all! *Brain Zapped* made a decent showing at film festivals in 2006, but it was never picked up by a network, which was a little disappointing for Selena. She has always loved reading and she thought the show had a great message. Luckily for Selena fans, the pilot is available on DVD for anyone who wants to see it!

After *Brain Zapped* didn't pan out, Selena began to feel that she may have outgrown all of the acting opportunities in Texas, but she wasn't ready to give up on her dream. She had finished up her stint on *Barney & Friends* in 2005, and Selena was really looking for another series. She loved working on a regular series, but for her next project, Selena was hoping to be the star. So when she heard about an open casting call in Austin for the Disney Channel, she begged her mother to take her. It was the smartest move Selena ever made.

In the meantime, Demi was keeping busy, too. Demi's older sister Dallas had been pursuing a music career for a number of years and Demi was very inspired by that. She had a big voice just like her big sister, and Demi definitely wanted a music career of her own. So, when Demi was eleven, she learned to play the piano and the guitar. She had always loved writing poetry, and once she knew how to play music, Demi quickly put the two together. She began writing songs and it was clear that Demi had a natural talent for it. Anything that was going on in her life got channeled into her music. Demi's agent and some of Dallas's producers knew a good thing when they heard it, and they quickly got Demi into the studio. She recorded a few of the songs she had written, including "Moves Me," and then she went on the road with Dallas. When Demi wasn't filming for *Barney & Friends* in 2004 and 2005, she joined her sister on a special USO tour. Dallas and Demi performed for U.S. troops at military bases across the country. Dallas was the bigger performer of the two, but Demi learned a lot about entertaining a large crowd, moving onstage, and singing live on that tour.

Then in 2005, when Demi was thirteen, she auditioned for a fun hip-hop dance instructional DVD and booked the job. The DVD was called Off Da Hook F-Troop Style and was produced by Well Go USA Productions. It featured choreographer Fenton "F-Troop"

Fulgham teaching five hip-hop routines with easy-to-follow steps. In addition to dancing, Demi also performed her song "Moves Me" on the DVD with a team of backup dancers. Demi had always loved to dance, so getting to teach other kids how to dance was very rewarding to her—and it didn't hurt that they were all learning to dance to her music!

Shortly after *Off Da Hook* was released, Demi and Selena finished their time on *Barney & Friends.* Demi went on a few auditions after that, but she didn't book anything and she was getting pretty frustrated. So Demi quit taking acting classes and focused on her music instead. She wrote more songs and continued to work on her vocals and playing guitar and piano. But, after a while, Demi really missed acting. She loved music and dancing, but there was also something about acting that she couldn't live without. It was hard for Demi to have faith in herself after so many disappointing auditions, but she knew she was talented and that if this was her dream, she had to have confidence in her own abilities to make it. So Demi went back to her acting classes and became more determined than ever to succeed as an actress. She worked hard and immediately began booking jobs. She did voice-overs for national radio and television commercials and became the official "Hitclips" spokesgirl for Hasbro. Hasbro had released a special music player that only played microchips called "Hitclips." Each Hitclip contained a few, kid-friendly versions of songs from popular artists. Demi did all of the voice-over work for the Hitclips commercials.

Next, Demi booked a guest role on the Emmy- and Golden-Globe-nominated Fox series *Prison Break*. She had a small part playing Danielle Curtin in the episode "First Down," which premiered on September 11, 2006. *Prison Break* tells the story of a man sentenced to death for a crime he didn't commit and his brother's elaborate plan to break him out of prison to save his life. The show has lots of action and adventure, and it is a favorite with viewers across the nation. It was pretty cool for Demi to get to see herself on such a popular show! After *Prison Break*, Demi landed a role on a much more kid-friendly series—Nickelodeon's *Just Jordan*. *Just Jordan* tells the story of Jordan, a young boy who has just moved from Arkansas to California, and all of the messes he gets into. Demi played Nicole in an episode entitled "Slippery When Wet." The episode first aired on November 17, 2007. In the episode, Jordan's best friend Tony has a crush on Demi's character, which meant she spent a lot of time with the guys on the set. Demi had a blast hanging out on the set with Little JJ, the young comedian who plays Jordan, especially since he constantly had her cracking up between takes.

Working on *Just Jordan* really made Demi realize just how much she wanted to work on shows and movies that kids her own age watched. So Demi continued to audition, but she focused most of her energy on parts on shows for kids and teens. She and Selena really encouraged each other during that time. They were both looking for just the right projects to help establish them as actresses and they weren't going to stop until they found them. Luckily, neither of them would have to wait very long!

CHAPTER 4
DISNEY COMES KNOCKING

When Selena was twelve, she got the opportunity that would change her life forever. Disney, one of the biggest names in the entertainment world, was holding open casting calls across the country looking for new talent, and they were holding one audition in Austin, Texas. So Selena and her mother packed up their car and made the four-hour drive to Austin. It was a huge opportunity for Selena, but she also knew that she would have to compete against thousands of other girls, so it was a little nerve-racking.

Luckily, Selena was up for the challenge. She went into the audition and wowed the casting agents with her spunk and raw talent. They were so impressed that they asked Selena to fly to California and audition for Disney executives. "They flew us out to California. It was definitely scary. I was in this room full of executives and I was testing against girls who have done movies," Selena explained to *Variety*. Selena was up against some pretty stiff competition, but the one thing that has always made her stand out in a crowd is her professional demeanor and her ability to deliver when the pressure is on. Selena nailed the audition, as usual. One of the executives overseeing Selena's audition was Gary Marsh, the president of entertainment for Disney Channel Worldwide. Gary is in charge of casting and developing new series for the Disney Channel. Gary told *Entertainment Weekly* that Selena's audition was "green, it was rough—but she had that It Factor." Gary had a knack for recognizing talent when he saw it, and he saw Selena as the next big Disney phenomenon. "We don't look at television as the endgame," he explained to *Entertainment Weekly*. "That's the launchpad . . . We go into this thinking we are going to build a star; it's not thinking we are casting a role." Selena could act, sing, and dance fairly well. She was a triple threat and Gary and the rest of the Disney executives wanted her to become a part of the Disney family.

Disney offered Selena the title role of Stevie in a pilot for a spin-off of the hit Disney series *Lizzie McGuire*, called *What's Stevie Thinking?* The new show starred Lalaine, a veteran Disney star from the hit show *Lizzie McGuire*. Sassy Lalaine played Lizzie's best friend, Miranda Sanchez, on the show. *What's Stevie Thinking?* followed Miranda Sanchez as she started high school at a new school away from her old friends. Stevie was Miranda's little sister, and a lot of the show centered on how the two sisters interacted with each other. Selena was incredibly excited to win the role, especially since she'd been a huge fan of *Lizzie McGuire*. Another reason Selena was thrilled to be a part of the cast was that *What's Stevie Thinking?* was going to be the first Disney Channel series to star a Hispanic family. Selena had always been a little disappointed that there weren't very many girls on television who looked like her, or families that celebrated the same holidays and traditions that her family did. Getting the opportunity to bring her culture to a mainstream television audience was very appealing to Selena. She had a great time shooting the pilot and working with the cast and crew. They were all very proud of the pilot, but unfortunately test audiences weren't as receptive to the show as Disney executives had hoped. After showing the pilot to several groups of kids who weren't that into it, Disney decided not to pick up the series.

Selena was disappointed that *What's Stevie Thinking?* hadn't taken off, but the pilot had done one thing—it had generated a lot of buzz about Selena in Hollywood, and soon Nickelodeon, Disney's biggest rival network, came calling. Selena took several meetings with their talent agents and even auditioned for a Nickelodeon pilot and a made-for-television movie. But it didn't really feel right to Selena. "It was uncomfortable," she explained to *Entertainment Weekly*, "like I was cheating on Disney." Disney had discovered Selena and she felt at home there. Luckily, Disney didn't feel any better about Selena possibly switching to Nickelodeon than Selena did! They quickly offered her roles in two new pilots, knowing that they would pick up at least one of them for sure. "That's a question of betting on talent," Gary Marsh explained to *Variety*. "Once you find the person, you've got to make a commitment to give them work to get their shot." Disney was dedicated to making Selena a star and both of the new pilots she shot were good fits for her. "Disney was like,

'Let's put you in everything we have,'" Selena's mother told *Entertainment Weekly*.

The first new pilot was a spin-off of *The Suite Life of Zack and Cody*. Disney went through a number of names for the series, including *Arwin!* and *Housebroken*. That show starred Arwin, the maintenance man from the Tipton Hotel. In the show, he moves in with his sister to help her look after her kids. Selena played one of Arwin's nieces, Chloe. Unfortunately, that show didn't test well with audiences and Disney decided to green-light the second pilot Selena had shot that year instead. That pilot was for a whimsical show about a family with magical powers called *Wizards of Waverly Place*. *Wizards of Waverly Place* was set in New York City and it explored the idea of modern teenage wizards using magic to get in and out of trouble. Selena's character was Alex, the only girl in the family, and easily the most mischievous character on the show. Selena had a blast filming the pilot and she immediately clicked with the rest of the cast. After filming was completed, Selena flew back home to Texas and waited for news, but she didn't have to wait long. *Wizards of Waverly Place* tested incredibly well, and soon Disney was signing Selena and the rest of the cast up for the first season of the show.

Selena was really looking forward to getting started with filming, but she was also a little sad. In order to accept her new role, Selena and her family would have to move to California. "The biggest challenge was moving away from home, and at first, I didn't know how I was gonna do it. Once I came out to L.A. and started working, I adjusted a little bit but I'm still a Texas girl. My escape is to go home and relax for a bit, which I get to do when we're on hiatuses," Selena explained to *Popstar!* It was a big risk to make that move. After all, Los Angeles is very different from little Grand Prairie, Texas! Selena's mom and stepfather didn't make a ton of money, and moving to Los Angeles was not going to be cheap. Luckily, Disney was willing to foot the bill in order to get Selena into the studio. They really believed in her. "Without Disney, we wouldn't be out here at all," Selena's mom explained to *Entertainment Weekly*. "We're a paycheck-to-paycheck family, and they kept paying for everything."

So Selena and her mom packed up the essentials and quickly moved to Los Angeles. It was a whirlwind, but Disney needed Selena in Hollywood as soon as possible, and she didn't want to make them wait. It was a big sacrifice for everyone. The family's entire life was in Texas—jobs, friends, school, and their home. Selena considered herself very lucky to have such a supportive mom and stepdad that were willing to do anything it took to help her achieve her dreams. "It was sad to say good-bye to my friends and family, but it was a happy moment, too. They were so proud of me for achieving my dreams," Selena told DiscoveryGirls.com. Selena's mom was able to run her production company from afar, but Selena's stepfather stayed behind with their home and four dogs to settle things in Texas before joining his family in California.

Disney helped Selena and her mom rent a huge loft in a newly renovated industrial building in downtown Los Angeles. It was just the sort of hip, cool apartment that anyone would expect the hottest new Disney star to live in, but Selena didn't have much time to settle in to her new place. Disney wanted to make sure that fans got a good dose of Selena before her show premiered. They booked her as a guest star on two of their most popular shows, *Hannah Montana* and *The Suite Life of Zack and Cody*, and she immediately began filming those spots. Selena's first guest role was as Cody's love interest on *The Suite Life of Zack and Cody*. The episode was called "A Midsummer's Nightmare" and in it all of the kids try out for a production of *A Midsummer Night's Dream*. Selena played Gwen, and her character was dating Cody. But when her character in the play has to kiss Zack's character in the play, it causes a whole host of problems. Gwen likes kissing Zack so much that she dumps Cody and the brothers get into a huge and very silly fight onstage during the play. It was a funny episode to film and it was also a big first for Selena as an actress—she got her first on-screen kiss in that episode! ". . . My first [on-screen kiss] was with Dylan Sprouse on *The Suite Life of Zack and Cody*. That was fun. He was shorter than me, so I had to bend down a little bit, but it was a cute episode," Selena told *Girls' Life Magazine*. Selena must have been pretty nervous before kissing such a cute boy in front of a huge audience of the cast and crew! She handled it well though, and even though there is no real romantic interest between Selena and either of the Sprouse twins, she remains good friends with Cole and Dylan.

Next Selena moved on to *Hannah Montana*, where she played Hannah's biggest rival for pop superstardom, Mikayla, an up-and-coming pop diva set on stealing all of Hannah's fans. Selena had a blast playing mean girl Mikayla. She was sweet when cameras were rolling or fans were around, but she morphed into a competitive, smack-talking diva when she was alone with Hannah. Selena got to do some pretty funny scenes and wear some super-funky clothes as part of her role. It was a really fun part to play, and fans loved her so much that Selena ended up guest starring on quite a few episodes as she battled Hannah for fans, the cute boy, and awards. She and Miley Cyrus, the show's star, who plays Miley Stewart and Hannah Montana, became good friends during filming. The two girls loved goofing around, talking about clothes and boys, and just generally being teenage girls together on set. As the two girls' friendship grew though, it became harder for Selena to be mean to Miley during filming. "Me and Miley [Cyrus of *Hannah Montana*] would do a scene where we're mad and saying mean things, and when they'd cut, we would run up to each other and say, 'I'm so sorry.' People would laugh and they're like, 'You're just acting,' and we're like, 'I know, but I feel so bad,'" Selena explained to *Girls' Life Magazine.* The cattiness between Miley and Selena was all acting, but their friendship was definitely real. The two girls are still the best of friends and, since they are both part of the Disney family, they see each other all the time at Disney events, premieres, and parties.

With two high-profile guest spots under her belt, Selena was more than ready to move on to her own starring role. She had been waiting for the opportunity to headline her own show for years and she wasn't about to waste the opportunity. Once she walked onto the *Wizards of Waverly Place* set, she blew everyone away with her spunk, talent, and professionalism, and executives knew right away that they had a hit on their hands! Selena had finally arrived—and Disney would never be the same.

CHAPTER 5
THE BELL RINGS FOR DEMI

While Selena was wowing executives at Disney, Demi was hanging out back in Texas. She had landed a number of small roles and plenty of voice-over and modeling work, but she was feeling a little discouraged that she wasn't out in Los Angeles with her best friend. Luckily, Selena wanted her best friend out in L.A. as much as Demi wanted to be there. Disney is always looking out for the next big thing, and when they began casting a new short series, *As the Bell Rings*, Selena made sure Demi heard about it. *As the Bell Rings* is an experimental short television series based on *Quelli dell'Intervallo*, a series that airs on Disney Channel Italy. The show features six best friends named Tiffany, Danny, Charlotte, Toejam, Brooke, and Skipper, and it explores what happens in the hallways of a high school in the five minutes between classes each day.

Demi was up for the role of Charlotte or Brooke. Charlotte is a music-obsessed, girl-next-door type. She's pretty, talented, and she likes Danny, while Brooke is a supersmart cutie who has an opinion about everything and a huge crush on Toejam. The role of Tiffany wasn't right for Demi. Tiffany is the stereotypical dumb blonde and the most popular girl in school. Since casting agents were looking for a bubbly blonde to play Tiffany, Demi didn't go out for the role—she wanted to keep her hair its natural color! Of the male characters, Skipper is the funny one and he always has a plan for any situation, although they usually backfire! Skipper has a major crush on Tiffany, but she hasn't ever seemed to notice. Toejam is the rational one and he often gets teased for being a nerd. And Danny is the cutie of the group. He's really into music and he has a serious crush on Charlotte, but he is always too nervous to ask her out.

Casting agents were looking for wholesome, attractive, and relatively unknown kids to fill the six roles. Demi knew she was going to be up against some serious competition and she worked for hours with her acting coach, Cathryn Sullivan, the day before she flew to Los Angeles for her screen test. She was very nervous before the audition and even wondered if she was "Disney" enough for the show. But after a very intense day of practice, Demi was more than ready and determined to get the part. She nailed the audition and was cast as Charlotte. Gabriella Rodriguez was cast as Brooke, and Carlson Young, who is also from Texas, was cast as Tiffany. Gabriella and Carlson were both sweet and fun to be around and Demi enjoyed working with them from their first rehearsal on. But what was really fun was meeting the adorable boys cast on the show. Tall and freckled Collin Cole was chosen to play Skipper, goofy Seth Ginsberg was cast as Toejam, and supercute Tony Oller was cast as Danny, Demi's love interest on the show. Seth and Demi had actually gone to the same acting coach back in Texas for a long time, so it was great for them to be able to work together again. There was plenty of silliness and flirtation between the kids on the set, but none of it was serious. They are all just very good friends. The show was shot in Austin, Texas, which was especially nice for Demi since it was close to all of her friends and family.

As the Bell Rings premiered on August 26, 2007, at 8:05 and 8:55 P.M. eastern standard time, and viewers loved it. It was the perfect mini-break between Disney's regular series. The five-minute scripts were funny and silly and they were about things that all high-school kids deal with like crushes, homework, teasing, and popularity. The cast shot fifteen episodes for the first season. Disney was very impressed with Demi's performances. Fans loved her down-to-earth attitude and her singing voice.

While on break from shooting, Demi auditioned for several Disney original made-for-television movies and a few full-length series pilots. After booking some of those jobs, Demi had to leave the cast of *As the Bell Rings*. She was doing so much work on other projects that she no longer had time to film the short series. Demi was replaced by spunky actress Lindsey Black, who signed on for twenty-five episodes. Demi was very sad to leave her *As the Bell Rings* costars behind, but she was excited about her future projects and she knew that they would stay friends. Besides, Seth and Carlson both live in Texas so it is easy for her to see them when she is home. Plus, the entire cast is so talented that Demi was pretty sure she'd get the chance to work with them again in the future!

CHAPTER 6
JUST LIKE MAGIC

Fans now know Selena as the star of the Disney Channel original series *Wizards of Waverly Place*, but she wasn't just handed that part—Selena had to audition just like everyone else. When Selena walked into the auditions, executives were expecting something special, and that is exactly what they got. They'd all seen Selena's work at previous auditions and in previous pilots, so they knew how talented she was, but they were blown away by just how incredible her audition was. Selena was reading for the part of Alex, the middle child and only girl in a family of modern-day wizards, for the show. "I wanted to try something different, so I went in there and presented them with my way with Alex. She's very spunky. I didn't want her to be a kind of girly girl. So she's the very Converse-wearing, outgoing one, always getting in trouble and getting her brothers in trouble as well," Selena explained to the *OC Register*. Selena brought a very funky, cool edge to the role and it was exactly what producers had been looking for. They cast her immediately. "I was ecstatic, but I was nervous and scared, too. I felt a little bit of everything," Selena told DiscoveryGirls.com. It was a perfect role for Selena and she really got into her new character before filming the pilot. The pilot was a hit at Disney and they ordered a full season worth of episodes, much to the delight of the cast and crew.

Wizards of Waverly Place is the story of the Russo family, who live on Waverly Place in New York City. The family owns and runs a sandwich shop, and is a lot like any other New York family, except that all three of the children in the family are wizards! Eventually, one of the three kids will be chosen to be the family wizard and the other two children will lose their powers, but until that day, all three of the kids can do magic. The kids are Justin, played by David Henrie, Alex, played by Selena, and Max, played by Jake T. Austin. Justin is the oldest and the most responsible, but he's also a little bit of a nerd. Alex is the middle child and only girl. She's spunky and popular, and is always game to use her magic for a quick fix. Max is the youngest and he's not quite as smart as his brother and sister. He's very goofy and he can't do as advanced magic as his brother and sister. Jerry Russo, played by David DeLuise, is their father, and he had magical powers until his brother was chosen as the family wizard. Jerry teaches his kids their magic lessons, but since he doesn't have powers, he can't always help when their spells go awry. Theresa Russo, the mom, is played by Maria Canals-Barrera. She is Mexican in heritage and she is the one who teaches her children about the importance of their heritage and their family. Since *What's Stevie Thinking?* didn't ever make it onto the air, *Wizards of Waverly Place* became the first Disney series to feature a Hispanic family. The Russos are a mix of Mexican and Italian, and the show really plays up the unique aspects of both of those cultures. The other regular character on the show is Harper, Alex's best friend. Harper is played by Jennifer Stone, and she and Selena are good friends in real life, too!

The show's writers and producers really made the cast a big part of the development process. They wanted Selena's opinion on her character, and she was more than happy to give it. "I asked that they keep her [Alex] edgy," Selena explained to *Entertainment Weekly*. "I don't want to be wearing heels. She wears Converse, and she's cool. I'm not really a girly girl." The show's writers were very impressed with Selena and they actually worked to make Alex a little like her, but with some key differences, of course! The writers needed their main character to be a little bit more of a troublemaker than Selena has ever been. "Alex is more outgoing and spunky. I'm definitely outgoing but I don't get into as much trouble. She usually breaks the rules and I'm pretty much a good girl. When it comes to clothes, I'm a huge Converse girl—I have so many pairs—and in the show, that's all my character wears!" Selena explained to DiscoveryGirls.com. Selena's favorite part about Alex is "probably that she's always getting into trouble and she's doing stuff that I wish I could do. At the end of the day it's all fake! I don't want to get in trouble and make a mess, but it's nice to pretend that it was real!" she explained to *Teen* magazine.

Alex definitely gets herself into some serious hot

water in some of Selena's favorite episodes. "The Quinceañera episode was probably my favorite, or the episode where Alex wanted to go to a rated R movie. She tries to put a spell on herself to magically go into the movie theater, but she ends up actually IN the movie, so she's stuck in this scary movie sorority-house flick, and they shot it just like a movie. It was so much fun because it was like being able to shoot an actual scary movie," Selena told PBSKids. org. Luckily, Alex always has her brothers and her parents to help bail her out of even the most bizarre magical situations!

The show's magical premise means that Selena has come to expect the unexpected on set. There are a lot of cool magical special effects and Selena has become a pro at working with interesting props and strange sets. "I think it's cool to sort of step into something supernatural," she explained to *Teen* magazine. Before landing the role of Alex, Selena had never actually been much a fan of fantasy. She'd never even read the *Harry Potter* books or seen the movies! "Our show's not as dark. It's lighter and it's a sitcom, so it's funny. We try to get in trouble, and, of course, with magic it's easy to get into trouble," Selena told *Teen* magazine. These days, Selena is pretty knowledgeable when it comes to the supernatural. If she had magic in real life she knows exactly what she would do. "Clone myself! Just to get out of class, it would be nice," she laughingly said to *Teen* magazine. But it's not the cool effects that are her favorite part of filming *Wizards of Waverly Place*, as she explained to PBSKids.org. "My favorite scenes are ones where all of the family is together. Whether it's a funny or dramatic scene, whether we're trying to solve a problem or doing magic or turning my brother invisible, it comes off best when we're with the whole family in the loft. I think when we're all together the show is at its strongest point. And I love being with the entire cast in a scene."

The *Wizards of Waverly Place* cast has definitely come together over the course of filming, especially Selena, Jennifer, Jake, and David. Selena considers her television brothers to be some of her best friends, so getting to hang out with them on set all day is a lot of fun for her. "I can't even explain it! I am very confident when I say that we are the closest cast Disney Channel has ever had. We've been told that because we spend every waking moment with each other—it's insane! Jake [Austin], Jen [Stone], David [Henrie], and I do karaoke together, we go to the movies, and we go surfing every weekend. And as soon as we get off work, we text and call each other. My mom is always like, 'You act like you never see each other!' We've just gotten so close," Selena told DiscoveryGirls.com. Hanging out with David and Jake has been eye-opening for only child Selena. It's the first time she's ever gotten to really experience what it would be like to have brothers, and she loves it. "They [David Henrie and Jake T. Austin] basically ARE my brothers; they're my real family. My mom laughs at me all the time because we're constantly in touch with one another off the set, we're always calling. They're always there for me, and it's torture when I can't see them every day. We do fight like brothers and sisters sometimes, but mostly we play around and joke around. I don't have any real life siblings so this way I can have brothers," Selena told PBSKids.org. "They're both so protective of me. Even when I like a boy or something, they have to make sure he's okay, or the boy has to be 'approved' by them." The closeness Selena, Jake, and David have developed offscreen definitely translates well into on-screen chemistry. They really seem like siblings, and their on-screen parents bonded with them fairly quickly as well. "It's been so much fun just to develop a new family and to have new friends. They're my second family, and everyone on there is so nice and so sweet. They're my real brothers and second parents!" Selena explained to *Teen* magazine.

When the stars aren't filming a scene, they work with their on-set tutor. David is already finished with high school, but Selena, Jen, and Jake all have to do a certain number of hours worth of classes everyday. Once her schoolwork is finished, Selena can relax for the rest of the day. She texts and e-mails her friends from her trailer, gossips with Jen, and shoots hoops with Jake. "We actually have one [a basketball court] on set. It's fun," Selena told *Girls' Life Magazine*. "I only take on [my TV brother], so when I beat him it's not a good feeling. He's only 12, and half the time he beats me."

Everyone also enjoys just sitting around and talking, as Selena explained to *Girls' Life Magazine*. "Well, David has these cards with questions like, 'Would you treat your kids the way your parents treat you?' They're conversation cards, and you can ask each other what's your embarrassing moment and stuff. Other than that, we talk and laugh. If we're tired, we all just lounge together. David likes to hit the back of my knee so I almost trip. He's always doing that. We just get silly and play patty-cake or something." And when Selena's not in front of the camera, she really enjoys watching the rest of the cast film their scenes. She's learned a lot from watching the show's other actors handle different scenarios.

Selena also loves getting the chance to see the live audience react for the first time to the comedic elements the cast has been rehearsing all week before the live taping. Selena adores getting to perform in front of the audience and she is so grateful for the fans who come out to watch the tapings. "I've worked with adults who are far more difficult than anybody in my cast right now," Peter Murrieta, the *Wizards of Waverly Place*'s executive producer, said to the *OC Register*.

"I've seen Selena stand back by the doorway when they load the audience out at the end of the night, thanking everybody for coming. They are more gracious and professional and friendly than a lot of grown-ups I've worked with."

Before the show was even on the air, Selena and the rest of the cast made fans out of everyone who came to watch their tapings. "It was actually a surprise because I didn't think I'd have fans until the show came out. But Jake and I have been stopped before. They'll say, 'We went to one of your tapings!' It's such a cool feeling when fans come up to you because they're so excited and nervous. Meanwhile, I'm thinking, 'I'm more excited and nervous than you are right now!' It's pretty cool," Selena told DiscoveryGirls.com.

Selena was very proud of *Wizards of Waverly Place* and she couldn't wait for fans to see the final product, but she was also nervous about how they would react. She was terrified that no one would want to watch, but she also knew that if fans liked the show, her life was going to change drastically. Selena had always wanted to be a famous actress, but being famous also meant that she could never go back to being plain old Selena Gomez from Grand Prairie, Texas. "I'm scared," Gomez said to the *OC Register* this summer. "But when I hang out with Miley and see how other kids look up to her, how they get so excited just because they looked at her, I think that making the kids' day means a lot." Selena may have been frightened, but she was proud to think that she may be a role model for other girls who want to be actresses, especially other Hispanic girls. Disney was definitely confident that the show would be a hit *and* that Selena would be a great star and role model that fans could look up to. "It's very difficult to be a teenager, period," Peter Murrieta explained to the *OC Register*. "Without anything else, it's just a hard thing. When you add the possibility of becoming a star almost exactly overnight, it just makes it more stressful. What I can say about both Selena and Jennifer is that they are great people who have their heads on their shoulders right."

Peter was right to have confidence in his stars. When *Wizards of Waverly Place* premiered on October 12, 2007, it was a huge hit. Fans loved the quirky concept, magic, and family dynamic, but most of all, they loved Selena as Alex. Her sassy attitude and cool, sporty style won over fans immediately, and Selena couldn't have been more proud. The show's popularity continued to grow as each episode aired, and Disney was so pleased with the response that they announced they were picking the show up for a second season, and even had the writers put together an hour-long special that aired in April 2008. In the special, Alex and Justin go to summer school at Wiz Tech, a spoof of *Harry Potter*'s Hogwarts School for Witchcraft and Wizardry. Fans loved the funny, good-natured satire, and the special garnered a record number of viewers. Everyone was excited by the show's success, but no one was more pleased than Selena. She has been working toward this starring role for the past two years with Disney through lots of failures and disappointments, and it meant the world to her to finally prove to everyone that she had more than enough talent and star power to really make it. She was finally a bona fide star, and she was only going to get bigger and bigger. Even in Selena's wildest dreams, she couldn't have imagined just how big, how fast.

CHAPTER 7
ROCK OUT

Demi was very proud of Selena's new show and she really enjoyed being a part of the Disney family on *As the Bell Rings*, but Disney had something even bigger in mind for Demi. She was one of the girls they had in mind for a brand-new Disney Channel made-for-television movie that was originally called *Rock Camp Rules!* It was about a talented young singer/songwriter named Mitchie who gets the chance to go a special camp for performers. Demi immediately fell in love with the script. It seemed like the part of Mitchie had been written just for her! The film called for a young actress who could sing, dance, act, and had real stage presence—Demi had all of those things!

Demi wowed the casting agents with her audition. She owned the stage and Disney executives knew as soon as she performed for them that they had found the perfect girl for the part. They offered Demi the role of Mitchie, and she accepted. Then she got some news that made everything even better—rock sensations the Jonas Brothers had been cast as her costars! She probably screamed with excitement for an hour! After all, the Jonas Brothers are one of the hottest teen rock acts to come out in a very long time, and all three of the brothers are absolutely adorable. Who wouldn't want to shoot a film with them? Nick, Joe, and Kevin Jonas are three brothers who perform together as a band. That have a platinum-selling album, several hit singles, and have toured the country both alone and with Miley Cyrus/Hannah Montana.

The Jonas Brothers were going to be playing the fictional boy band Connect 3 in the series. "The one thing that really drew us toward it was the music," Nick Jonas told the *Orlando Sentinel*. "We listened to the songs. We thought the music was something that was really interesting to us. Especially the song we did with the band Connect 3. That's maybe a song that we would do one day. So it all kind of worked out. It was good." Joe had the largest role of Shane Gray, the lead singer of Connect 3 who has a major anger management problem. "Joe did an incredible job of playing the disgruntled rock star," Gary Marsh, the president of entertainment for Disney Channel Worldwide, explained to the *Orlando Sentinel*. "If you meet Joe, you know that's not who he is. He's the kindest, gentlest soul in the world." Kevin took on the role of funny, goofy Jason and Nick played serious Nate, and neither of those roles was too much of a stretch for the boys. "My character is out there, a little spacey, but I love it. I get to be a little loopy, and it's kind of fun. Nick plays the leader in the group, which is really true. He always keeps me in line—me and Joe are always joking around. I'm always just having a good time; Joe is goofing off. Joe's nickname is 'Danger.' Nick is like, 'OK, guys.' We're just like, 'Whatever,'" Kevin told *Girls' Life Magazine*. Nick agreed, as he explained to *Girls' Life Magazine*. "My character in the movie, his name is Nate, and he's a lot like me in the sense that he knows what he wants and knows he has to keep his head on straight. He's got a clear picture of what has to happen with the band, and he doesn't lose his focus. He's kind of the exact opposite of Kevin's character Jason. The dynamic there is really cool."

With the Jonas Brothers signed on, the rest of the roles were cast. Alyson Stoner, who has appeared in films like *Cheaper by the Dozen* and Disney shows including *Phineas and Ferb* and *The Suite Life of Zack and Cody*, won the role of Caitlyn and Meaghan Martin, Jasmine Richards, and Anna Maria Perez de Tagle were cast as the camp's mean girls. Luckily, the mean girls weren't really mean. Demi and Meaghan are actually really good friends and they hang out together all the time! One of the coolest casting decisions, at least to Demi, was when Maria Canals-Barrera, who plays the role of Theresa Russo on *Wizards of Waverly Place*, was cast as Mitchie's mother in the movie. That meant that Selena and Demi were going to be sharing an on-screen mom!

With the cast in place, the writers made some final tweaks to the script and renamed the project *Camp Rock*. The final version is sort of a rock-and-roll Cinderella story. Mitchie Torres is a talented singer and songwriter who desperately wants to spend the summer at a rock-and-roll camp, but her family can't afford it. So Mitchie's mom gets a job as the camp cook and negotiates a deal for her daughter: Mitchie is allowed to attend camp as long as she helps out in the kitchen between classes and during free time. Mitchie agrees and soon she's off at camp.

It's especially cool to be at Camp Rock that year because the members of Connect 3, one of the hottest pop bands ever, are at camp working as counselors. They used to go to Camp Rock every summer as campers. Connect 3's lead singer, Shane, has developed a bad attitude and keeps throwing fits onstage. So the rest of the band decides that they are all going back to Camp Rock to try to come together again as a band. "Shane is not happy he's going there," Kevin Jonas explained to *Girls' Life Magazine*. "We canceled our summer tour, and he's got to find himself again. We know this will be good for him no matter how much he hates it." Even if Connect 3 isn't psyched to be at camp, Mitchie certainly is. She loves it there and becomes fast friends with Caitlyn, who dreams of being a music producer, but clashes with mean girls Tess, Peggy, and Ella. Things get a little complicated when Mitchie feels ashamed and embarrassed that her mother is working in the kitchen. She lies and claims to be from a wealthy family while hiding her kitchen duties from her new friends.

While working on a new song, Mitchie is overheard by Shane Gray, the lead singer of Connect 3, but he never sees who she is. He is totally inspired by her singing and sets out trying to find her. But it's not easy since everyone has discovered Mitchie's lies and she isn't even going to her classes. Eventually Mitchie, with the help of her mom and her real friends, realizes that she can be herself and that her real strength lies in her own unique voice and perspective. She and Shane Gray strike up a romance and she helps him find his voice as she discovers hers. Mitchie rocks out as herself in her final camp performance and totally steals the show.

Demi was thrilled with the final script and before she knew it, she was on her way to the set. Filming for *Camp Rock* took place in Ontario, Canada. They filmed at two camps, Camp Wanakita and Camp Kilcoo in the Haliburton Highlands. The locations were breathtaking, with lush grounds and a gorgeous lake. Demi felt right at home out in the wilderness. She'll always be a country girl at heart so she didn't miss the hustle and bustle of Los Angeles. It was also easier to get in tune with her character on location. The cast went through a lot of rehearsals together to get all of the musical numbers and dance sequences just right, and by the end of that they were all pretty good friends.

Demi must have been pretty nervous getting to know her supercute costars, Nick, Kevin, and Joe. She wasn't even sure that they would want to be friends! In fact, in the very first scene she filmed with Joe, Demi was covered in flour almost the entire time—not exactly how she had hoped to look the first time they worked together! Luckily, Joe thought it was pretty funny and the two warmed up to each other almost immediately.

But it wasn't quite as easy getting to know the other two Jonas Brothers. "Nick's pretty shy," Demi explained to *M* magazine. "I thought Nick didn't like me at first because we didn't really talk, but that's just because it takes a while for him to warm up." But once they had spent some time together, the boys and Demi became very good friends. Her goofy personality and sense of humor made her too fun not to hang out with! And once she got to know the boys better, they went from being too-cool rock stars to just regular, albeit cute, boys in her head, just like Demi's guy friends at home. "Kevin is very protective and Joe is a funny dork!" Demi told *M* magazine about her *Camp Rock* costars. The boys and Demi definitely cracked each other up while filming. "I think sometimes when you forget your lines it's kind of a funny moment," Nick explained to *Girls' Life Magazine*. "That's what just happened in this last limousine scene. I was supposed to be saying something like, 'By the way, we told the press you'd be singing a duet with the winner at Final Jam,' and it came out like, 'By the way, winter's coming faster than summer so make sure you wear some pajamas,' or something like that. It was crazy."

Line flubs aside, Demi and her castmates were mostly working when they were on set, but they did have downtime too. The Jonas Brothers spent a lot of time in between takes practicing their kung fu moves on each other and wrestling. "We had kung fu training recently, and we were just kind of going over it, refreshing our minds of all this kung fu stuff. Once in a while, you'll see us kind of look like we're fighting, and we're just pretend fighting," Joe explained to *Girls' Life Magazine*. And when they weren't fighting, Joe could almost always be found flirting with the girls on set. Nick and Kevin might not be quite as flirty as their middle brother, but the boys do get a little competitive when it comes to the attention of girls. "No matter what, you're always trying to be smoother with the girls than your brother. There is that sense of, 'Dude, she likes me.' 'No, she definitely likes me.' We actually kind of go at it," Nick told to *Girls' Life Magazine*. Demi probably didn't mind flirting with the boys, and she always made sure to give them equal attention!

All of that behind-the-scenes flirting did come in handy, even if Demi and Joe are just friends. Their characters had an on-screen romance and their chemistry is undeniable. They even had a big kissing scene at the end of the film. It comes right after the final camp performance when they perform a big duet called "We Rock." It was Demi's first real on-screen romance, so she was probably pretty nervous when it came time to shoot that kiss. To prepare, "I think we both popped a breath mint!" Demi explained to *M* magazine. In the end, they pulled the kiss off beautifully. And even though Demi says she doesn't have feelings for Joe, it couldn't have been that bad to kiss such a hottie over and over again until they got it just perfect!

Unfortunately, not all of the scenes were as much fun to film as the kissing scene. There were plenty of scenes where Demi's character had to deal with some pretty embarrassing stuff. And, even though it was all acting, it couldn't have been easy for Demi to shoot. Luckily, Demi is a real professional. She handled all of her scenes gracefully and even gave the Jonas Brothers a few pointers. After all, *Camp Rock* was their first big acting gig! They'd played themselves before, but this was their first opportunity to take on fictional characters, and they were a little nervous, as Joe explained to the *Orlando Sentinel.* "It's so new to us. We're so used to performing onstage. I didn't know how I would do. Honestly, I got kind of nervous." But once the boys loosened up and really got into character, they had a blast with it. "I never thought about it, but I really loved acting," Kevin said the *Orlando Sentinel*. "Hopefully, we have a long future with the Disney Channel." Demi and the boys performed several songs in the film including solos, duets, and big group numbers. "We became part of it after the music was written, but it's fantastic," Kevin explained to *Girls' Life Magazine*. Both Demi and the Jonas Brothers really like to be involved with the songwriting process when it comes to their own music, but they were all impressed with the songs that had been created for *Camp Rock*. They were fun to perform and they really added to the overall feel and message of the movie, like Demi's solo "This is Real, This is Me," which cuts to the heart of the movie's message that it's okay to be yourself and that you should always be proud of who you are. Perhaps the biggest change for the Jonas Brothers was lip-synching during filming. They never do that in their concerts or music videos, as Joe explained to *Girls' Life Magazine*. "It's definitely new and weird because they have to do different takes. If they like one take, they have to sync it up perfectly. Having just the music playing is easier to do that with." Demi had to lip-synch her performances, too, but she already had some experience with voice-over work so she was a natural. The most difficult scene to lip-synch was the final performance of the song "We Rock," since it included so many cast members. But they nailed it, and it is a really fun number to watch.

By the end of filming, the cast wasn't ready to say good-bye. They had all had such a good time working together, on set and off. Between spontaneous parties, bonfires, and other fun stuff, it actually was a little bit like being at camp! "One night we had a dance party. We made up cheesy dances and we were running outside," Demi explained to *Popstar!* All of the actors have remained very good friends and they see one another often. Demi even went on vacation with Meaghan to Niagara Falls after filming wrapped! In the end, the whole cast was very proud of what they had accomplished. They knew the movie would look amazing and they were very excited about the message it would give fans—to always be proud of who you are. "It was a real confidence booster. My character and I both like to rock out and now we're not afraid to!" Demi told *Popstar!* Fans certainly got the message loud and clear. They went nuts over the film and there is already a talk of a sequel in the works, so maybe Demi, Nick, Kevin, Joe, Alyson, and Meaghan will all get to reunite for *Camp Rock 2* sometime soon!

CHAPTER 8
MAKING MUSIC

Demi certainly lit up that stage as singing-star-in-the-making Mitchie Torres, but in real life both Demi and her BFF Selena are well on their way to even more successful musical careers all their own. One of the things that attracted Disney to Selena and Demi was their ability to sing. Both girls had plenty of practice back when they were on *Barney & Friends*. Since then, however, the two have graduated to slightly more mature subject matter.

Selena was the first to get into the studio for Disney. She recorded "Everything Is Not What It Seems," the theme song for *Wizards of Waverly Place*. It's a quirky, upbeat pop song that fits the vibe of the magical show perfectly. Selena had a lot of fun recording the song, and she learned tons from that recording session. Recording a single isn't easy, especially for a relatively new singer like Selena. But, by the end of the session, the song was perfect. And Selena certainly loves hearing it at the start of her show!

Next Selena went back into the studio to record a cover of a classic Disney tune, "Cruella De Vil." Selena's version is a fun twist on the original tune from 1961. The song first appeared in the Disney animated film *101 Dalmatians* and was written about the story's villain, Cruella De Vil. It has long been a favorite of Disney fans and has been covered in the past by other young stars like Lalaine and Hayden Panettiere. For Selena's cover, producers added a little bit more of a modern beat so the result is a sassy groove that is sure to put listeners in a good mood—even if it is about a villain!

After the song was recorded, Selena took the music to a new level with an awesome video shoot. Selena performed the song on a giant runway. Her band, dressed all in black, was set up at the back of the runway and Selena strutted her stuff up and down the catwalk as she sang. She wore an adorable red button-down collared shirt, black vest, black skinny pants, a black-and-white polka-dotted scarf and a patent-leather red swing coat. That was intercut with scenes from the animated classic and scenes of Selena singing alone in front of a black-and-white polka-dotted background. In those scenes she's wearing a black sequined minidress with black pants, a short black jacket, a big red ribbon bracelet, black Converse sneakers, and a supercool black hat with a big red ribbon on it. The video was totally chic and it played often on the Disney Channel. Selena's favorite part to film was when she got to interact with a crowd while she sang on the runway. Wowing an audience is why she likes singing so much. "I think you can be more of yourself when you're singing. You can have a little bit more control over it. It's a different process, with going into the studio and not having to worry about what you look like on camera. You write music and perform it, have fun, then go on concert and jam out in front of an audience," Selena told PBSKids.org. Selena's video was featured on the special *101 Dalmations* platinum-edition DVD that was released on March 4, 2008.

Just when Selena thought it couldn't get any cooler, she found out that her version of "Cruella De Vil" was featured on *Disneymania, Vol. 6*, a compilation CD that Disney puts out every year featuring hot new singers and bands covering classic songs. Selena's tune made the cut along with the Plain White T's, Drew Seeley, the Cheetah Girls, Nikki Blonsky, Jordan Pruitt, and Demi! Demi's song for *Disneymania, Vol. 6* was a little more modern than Selena's pick. It was a cover of the Academy Award nominated tune "That's How You Know" from 2007's *Enchanted*. *Enchanted* tells the story of an animated princess who is magically transported into the real world, where she learns a lot of about life, love, and happiness. The film stars Amy Adams and Patrick Dempsey and it dominated the 80th Academy Awards, where three of its songs were nominated for Best Original Song. "That's How You Know" didn't win the award, but it's still a fan favorite. Demi was honored to get to record it for *Disneymania, Vol. 6*. But it wasn't just a copy of the sweet song. Demi's version has a serious rock-and-roll edge to it. Fans loved that she had made the song her own.

The bigwigs at Hollywood Records were just as impressed with Demi's vocal abilities as her fans were.

Rumors of her killer performances in *Camp Rock* had reached them and her cover of "That's How You Know" was even more impressive. Hollywood Records, which is owned by Disney, signed Demi to a record deal in early 2008. Demi had never been more excited. Putting out an album and touring has always been one of her biggest dreams and signing with Hollywood brought her one step closer to achieving just that. Demi had been writing songs for a quite a while so she already had some material. She worked with producers to polish some of her songs and perfect them for her album, but she also paired up with some old friends to write new material—the Jonas Brothers! The boys had come to respect Demi so much while filming *Camp Rock* that they were absolutely thrilled to be asked to help her with her album. Demi and Nick usually laid down the foundations for each of the songs together and then got Joe and Kevin's help fixing and tweaking the song to perfection. Nick usually came up with the chords while Demi was the creative genius behind the lyrics. "[Demi] has an amazing voice, and she's a great actress and has become a good friend of ours. We're writing with her for a record she'll probably release at the end of the year," Joe told *USA Today*.

Demi was ready to hit the studio to start recording her album in early spring 2008. It was a lot of hard work and late nights, but in the end, Demi was so proud of her album. It was exactly the record she'd always dreamed of putting out, and she couldn't wait to share it with her fans. Unfortunately, the album wasn't set to be released until fall 2008. Demi and her fans couldn't wait that long, so Disney set Demi up with a special concert for the media and executives from Disney and Hollywood Records to show her off and get the ball rolling. They called the show "The Next Big Thing" and it took place during a big annual Disney meeting in April 2008 in New York City. It was Demi's first trip to New York and she was nervous and excited and a little awestruck, but she managed to shake her nerves before the show. There, Demi performed the ballad "This is Real, This is Me" from *Camp Rock* while sitting alone onstage playing the piano. Demi played up her unique rock chic vibe with black skinny jeans with suspenders that she let hang by her sides, a black-and-white plaid button-down shirt, flats, and a funky black hat. Her look and sound really set her apart from some of the more recent Disney singing stars like Miley Cyrus and Hilary Duff, which is exactly what Demi was going for. She wanted to stand out and prove to everyone at Disney that she had the new, fresh star power that they had been looking for.

Hollywood Records got the message loud and clear—Demi was ready to hit the scene! So they sent her on tour with the Jonas Brothers for summer 2008. It was the Jonas Brothers' first big tour as headliners and it was called "Burning Up," which was particularly appropriate since Demi plus the Jonas Brothers was a pretty hot ticket! "Yeah, we're going to bring Demi on tour with us. She's our costar in the movie *Camp Rock*. And we've been writing with her a lot for her record. It's going to be very exciting," Joe told JuniorCelebs.com. But the costars won't be performing any songs from *Camp Rock*. "Just our songs, just from our record," Kevin explained to *Girls' Life Magazine*. As much as everyone loves the music from *Camp Rock*, the Jonas Brothers and Demi wanted their fans to get the chance to hear and experience them as artists instead of as their characters from the movie.

The concert was supercool, and Demi loved being on the road with the boys. They had a lot of fun together exploring new cities and rocking out onstage every night. It always makes traveling more fun to have a good friend along for the ride, and Demi was extra thankful to have Joe, Nick, and Kevin with her since it was her first tour. She was much less nervous with the boys there to give her advice, tips, and to back her up. If only Selena could have come on tour, too, it would have been perfect! But Selena is in talks to possibly put an album out herself with Hollywood Records, so maybe she'll be opening up for Demi on her next tour. One thing is for sure; both Demi and Selena love music, so fans are sure to hear more of their beautiful voices soon.

CHAPTER 9
VIDEO REVOLUTION

In January 2008, Selena and Demi decided to give their fans a taste of what their friendship was really like behind the scenes. These two friends always have the best time together and they wanted everyone to see just what they mean to each other. Inspired by fellow Disney stars and the Jonas Brothers, Demi and Selena decided to make some videos for their fans. The Jonas Brothers have their own YouTube channel where they record and post videos of themselves goofing around on tour and at home. The boys wanted to give their fans a taste of what their lives are like behind the scenes. The Jonas Brothers' videos are funny and silly, and fans love them. Demi and Selena love them, too, and when the girls signed on to do a Disney Channel movie together, they wanted to give fans a sneak peek of production. However, once Demi and Selena started recording, the videos became a lot more than that. The Jonas Brothers gave Demi the idea for the videos on the set of *Camp Rock*. The videos were originally intended to be podcasts, which are special broadcasts designed specifically for use on Apple's iPods, but the girls decided that that format was a little limiting. They wanted all of their fans to see the videos—not just the ones with iPods—so they decided to post the videos on YouTube, a special website where anyone can post videos. Demi already had a YouTube channel, www.youtube.com/user/therealdemilovato, but she hadn't posted anything yet. Since that YouTube channel was already up and running, the girls posted their videos there. They shoot all of their videos on Selena's Apple laptop, usually in her room, but they also do some shooting on the road when they are off filming for extended periods of time.

The first video that Selena and Demi shot together was a message thanking fans for their continued support and announcing that the girls would be starring together in a new Disney Channel original movie, *Princess Protection Program*. In their second video, the girls demonstrated their secret handshake, which involved singing the Kit Kat candy jingle while doing some complicated clapping. Other videos showed Selena and Demi doing everything from dancing to a Miley Cyrus song, to giving shout-outs and birthday wishes to specific fans, to answering questions from fans. They revealed their favorite colors, that they both wear purity rings, silly things they've done, and some of their hopes for the future. The videos really give fans a chance to get to know the two girls behind their characters on Disney. Selena and Demi were totally silly on camera, and they reminded a lot of viewers of themselves and their friends just goofing around and being silly. It also gave fans a chance to get to know Demi and Selena's friends, like when the girls introduced buddy Samantha Droke's "Live in Love" T-shirt line, when Demi's little sister, Madison, made a guest appearance, and when the girls introduced some of their *Princess Protection Program* costars.

Some of Demi and Selena's friends got into the action themselves by making their own videos. *Hannah Montana* star Miley Cyrus and her friend Mandy make a series of YouTube videos that they call *The Miley and Mandy Show*. After watching a video where Demi and Selena talked about the Power Rangers and Demi's teeth and eye makeup, Miley and Mandy made a parody of the video. Miley pretended to be Selena and Mandy took on Demi's role. Instead of discussing the Power Rangers, Miley talked about *Teenage Mutant Ninja Turtles* and Mandy donned heavy eye makeup to mimic Demi. Selena and Demi thought Miley and Mandy's video was pretty funny. Alyson Stoner, one of Demi's costars from *Camp Rock,* took a different tactic. Instead of a parody, she issued a video challenge to the girls for a dance contest. Demi and Selena filmed a video response where they laughingly discussed their dance experiences on *Barney & Friends, Camp Rock*, and *Another Cinderella Story*. Demi and Selena are both good dancers, but they eventually asked Alyson to challenge them to some other type of contest since Alyson is a phenomenally talented dancer who teaches hip-hop dance classes and has been a featured dancer in a Missy Elliot music video! Hopefully Alyson will come up with another challenge that the girls are more willing to participate in.

All of the videos, whether goofy, serious, or simply

thankful, were wildly popular with Demi and Selena's fans. After only four months, the girls' YouTube channel had been viewed over 700,000 times and had over 50,000 subscribers. With that kind of response, Demi and Selena will probably be posting many, many more videos for their fans to watch soon—so keep an eye out for new ones!

CHAPTER 10
SILVER SCREEN SELENA

Selena absolutely loves working in television. Filming *Wizards of Waverly Place* every week has been a dream come true and Selena really has her character down. But working on the same show every week isn't always as challenging as Selena would like. Every once in a while, it's nice for her to try her hand at something new. Luckily, *Wizards of Waverly Place* doesn't film year-round. Selena has several months off at a time for vacation, and instead of taking it easy, energetic Selena uses that time to film movies when she can. She's only done a few so far, but she can't wait to do more.

Filming a movie is very different from filming a television show—the sets are bigger, the cameras are different, and it's a big change to film with people she's just met instead of the cast and crew she works with every single week at Disney. But all of that is very appealing to Selena. Doing films gives Selena a chance to play different types of characters and broaden her range as an actress.

Selena is very picky about the types of roles she takes on. She doesn't say yes to just anything! She wants to have a long career and be taken seriously as an actress, so she only accepts roles that she thinks will help her acting skills and appeal to her current fans. Selena actually turned down a starring role in *High School Musical 3*, the first feature film in the Disney *High School Musical* franchise. *High School Musical* is the most successful made-for-television movie of all time and it catapulted its stars, Zac Efron, Vanessa Hudgens, Ashley Tisdale, and Corbin Bleu, to superstardom. *"High School Musical 3* is cute, and I think it would be a great opportunity for someone else," Selena explained to the *New York Daily News.* "But I passed on it because I didn't want to do it. I plan to take other roles in acting that are challenging for me." Lots of other actresses would have loved to have been offered that part, but Selena didn't feel it was right for her. *High School Musical* fans were disappointed that Selena wasn't joining the cast, but at the end of the day Selena has to do what feels right for her. She can't take a role just because it will be a big hit. She has to take roles because they appeal to her, and it's really wonderful that she trusts her own judgment so much! It shows just how much confidence Selena has in herself and her abilities.

One role that did really appeal to Selena was providing the voice for Helga in *Horton Hears a Who!*, the smash hit animated film based on the classic Dr. Seuss story. "I had never done animation, so I thought it would be cool to try something different," Selena told the *New York Daily News.* Selena had long been a Dr. Seuss fan and she loved the story. "I remember reading his books like crazy with my grandmother when I was younger." *Horton Hears a Who!* is the story of an elephant named Horton who discovers an entire world of creatures called Whos existing on a daisy. Horton befriends one of the Whos, and decides it's up to him to keep them safe. Horton then goes through a series of dangerous and silly situations and eventually gets the Whos and their world to a safe spot. The film built upon the original story, expanding the characters and world and giving the story new life.

Getting the opportunity to bring one of her favorite

childhood books to life would be cool for anyone, but what made the film even cooler were her amazing costars. Famous comedians Steve Carell and Jim Carrey played the two largest roles in the film, the Mayor of Whoville and Horton, respectively. Selena played Steve Carell's daughters in the film—all ninety of them. They were all named Helga and, since they each had a unique look, Selena had to come up with a voice for each. "I voiced all of them," Selena explained to the *New York Daily News*. "I had to change up my voice to do higher voices, and then bring it down to do lower voices. All of the Mayor's daughters look different, so I play many different characters."

Selena was definitely excited to work alongside some of the biggest names in comedy, and she was ready to show them what she could do. Unfortunately, the complicated recording schedules meant that Selena never got to actually meet her on-screen dad, Steve Carell. They recorded in completely separate sessions, not that anyone can tell from the finished movie—it sounds like they were in the same room! Selena was a little disappointed. She had been looking forward to meeting the funny man. "It was kind of a bummer! But at the same time, it was cool. I can see him and say 'Hey, I played your daughter!' " Selena told the *New York Daily News*. Hopefully Selena will get the chance to act alongside Steve again—and this time actually come face-to-face with him!

The next role that Selena took on was completely different. She won the lead part of Mary in *Another Cinderella Story*. It was the follow-up film to 2004's *A Cinderella Story* starring Disney alum Hilary Duff and *One Tree Hill*'s Chad Michael Murray. "It is not the sequel to the first one with Hilary Duff," Selena explained to the *New York Daily News*. Instead, it's a take on the same basic premise—a modern version of the classic story of Cinderella. "At a ball, I meet a guy and we fall in love during a dance. Instead of dropping my glass slipper, I drop my MP3 player," Selena told the *New York Daily News*. Selena's character Mary is a hip-hop and tango dancer and over the course of the story she got to do some amazing dance sequences with her love interest in the film, Andrew Seeley, who played the part of Joey Parker.

Andrew was the singing voice for Zac Efron in Disney's *High School Musical* and he cowrote the Emmy nominated song "Get'cha Head in the Game" from the film. With Andrew's smooth voice, natural charisma, and dance experience, he was a natural fit for the role of Joey. Both Drew and Selena did some singing in *Another Cinderella Story*, much to the delight of Selena's fans.

Selena's role in *Another Cinderella Story* was one of her most mature to date. She got to play a high-school student and she got to have her first big-screen romance. Selena was a little nervous about the kissing scene before they shot it. Luckily, she and Drew became friends very quickly, and they had been filming together for weeks, so they were already pretty comfortable around each other by the time they shot that scene. "We haven't shot that [the kissing scene] yet, but I've been dancing with Drew for like three weeks. So I've known him really long. We've been rehearsing. It's so comfortable with him, so I don't think it's going to be too weird," Selena told *Girls' Life Magazine* before they had filmed the big scene. Filming romantic, flirty scenes with such a cutie was probably a lot of fun for Selena! And she got to show off her singing and dancing skills and try out a very different type of role. Mary was definitely spunky like Selena's *Wizards of Waverly Place* character Alex, but she was also a lot more focused and hardworking.

Another Cinderella Story was slated to premiere in theaters in April 2008, but the studio decided to release it straight to DVD instead, much to Selena's disappointment. She was looking forward to seeing herself up on the big screen, but she understood their decision. Financially, the film would do much better as a DVD release, and Selena knew her fans would buy copies, so she wasn't too bummed. It hit store shelves on September 4, 2008.

Selena has loved her first few experiences acting in feature films and she's definitely excited to do more, as long as the parts are right for her. Selena reads every script her agent sends her very carefully and always talks over her options with her mom and stepfather. She wants to make sure that her career is diverse and challenging, and she doesn't ever want her fans to get bored with the roles she

BEST FRIENDS FOREVER
SELENA GOMEZ
& DEMI LOVATO

DEMI PERFORMS
AT DISNEY'S THE
NEXT BIG THING.

DEMI POSES
FOR PICTURES.

SELENA STEALS SOME ICING FROM WIZARDS COSTAR DAVID HENRIE.

SELENA WAVES TO HER FANS.

SELENA POSES WITH MINNIE MOUSE AT THE
HIGH SCHOOL MUSICAL 2 PREMIERE.

DISNEY FRIENDS DAVID HENRIE, SELENA, CHELSEA STAUB, AND KEVIN, JOE, AND NICK JONAS.

LOOKING GORGEOUS!

SELENA GOES FOR A FUNKY LOOK AT THE MOVIES.

BOB INGER, DEMI, MADISON PETTIS, SELENA, AND JASON EARLES AT THE CHEVY EVENT.

SELENA ROCKS A 1980s GLAM LOOK AT A PREMIERE.

DAVID HENRIE CRASHES A PHOTO OF DEMI AND HER CAMP ROCK COSTARS MEAGHAN MARTIN, JASMINE RICHARDS, AND ANNA MARIA PEREZ DE TAGLE.

ROCK IT OUT! CAMP ROCK STARS: ANNA MARIA PEREZ DE TAGLE, KEVIN JONAS, MEAGHAN MARTIN, JOE JONAS, DEMI, AND NICK JONAS.

selects, so she tries to choose something new and different every time. Selena is also being very careful not to choose any roles that require her to do anything she isn't completely comfortable with. Selena will likely have the opportunity to be in films for years to come, so there is plenty of time for her to tackle all kinds of interesting parts in the future!

CHAPTER 11
PRINCESS PROTECTION PROGRAM

Life on the big screen is pretty sweet, but Selena and Demi's first love will always be television. They both grew up performing on TV together, so it was only a matter of time before they reunited to work on a television project together again. This time, instead of *Barney & Friends*, Demi and Selena were both cast in a fun and girly Disney Channel original made-for-television movie called *Princess Protection Program*. Demi won the role of Princess Rosie while Selena tackled the part of tomboy Carter.

When Princess Rosalinda's country is invaded by an evil dictator, she is sent to a safe location as part of the Princess Protection program, a secret agency dedicated to protecting princesses in danger. Rosalinda is sent to live with Mason, an agent in the program, and he and his daughter Carter help her pretend to be an ordinary teen named Rosie. Carter is an insecure tomboy who works at a local bait shop after school. Carter is a little bit of a social misfit, but she secretly dreams of going to the big school dance with her crush, Donnie, the hottest guy in town. Rosie is as at ease in social situations as Carter is awkward, and the two girls clash when Rosie quickly becomes the most popular girl in school. Eventually Carter teaches Rosie to be less of a prissy princess and Rosie helps Carter learn to be more of a lady. The characters were pretty true to life since Selena is more of a tomboy and Demi is more of a girly girl, but in real life the two have never had issues with each other like Rosie and Carter!

The plot of *Princess Protection Program* was funny and the script was very well written. Both of the main characters were well developed and challenging, so the girls were psyched when they heard the good news that they had both been cast in the film. Not only did it mean they had landed great roles, but it meant months of filming together on a beautiful set in tropical Puerto Rico. It was basically heaven for these two best friends. Thanks to their usually hectic schedules, Selena and Demi don't usually get to spend as much time together as they'd like, but they had adjoining trailers on set and rooms in the same hotel, so they had a lot of fun goofing off between takes and after filming. They got to rehearse together, do their schoolwork together, and hang out at the beach on their days off. The girls hadn't gotten to spend that much uninterrupted time together in years and they didn't want the filming to ever end.

In addition to all of the best friend togetherness, Demi and Selena made quick friendships with their castmates including Samantha Droke, Jamie Chung, and Robert Adamson. Robert played hunk Donnie, and Samantha and Jamie played some of the local mean girls who make Carter's life difficult, but in real life the entire cast got along really well. Samantha has been friends with Demi and Selena for a very long time and they are often seen sporting T-shirts she made that say "Live in Love" across the front of them. So the girls were pretty psyched when Sam joined the cast, even if Sam was playing the villain in the film. There were also a number of actors from Puerto Rico in the cast playing smaller roles and extras and they all had a great time together. The cast had dinner together, sing-alongs in the van on the way to and from the set, and made funny YouTube videos from their trailers.

It was definitely a silly set, right down to the crazy wrap party on the beach at the end of filming, where they had dancing, limbo, and a huge bonfire. The party was incredible, but it was also bittersweet, since it meant that Demi and Selena wouldn't get to see their new friends every day anymore. Saying good-bye to the cast and crew was really difficult, but at least Demi and Selena had promotional events and the premiere to look forward to for a cast reunion—plus a lot of the other actors were Disney regulars so they were pretty much guaranteed to see each other often. The movie premiered on September 19, 2008, and Demi and Selena's fans went nuts over it. Both girls gave stellar performances and their real-life best friend chemistry definitely translated on-screen. The film was such a success that there is almost bound to be another project starring these BFFs soon!

CHAPTER 12
BEST FRIENDS FOREVER

Demi and Selena will always be best friends, no matter what the future holds, and it's going to be a pretty great future if their fans have anything to say about it! These two starlets have been there for each other through thick and thin and they are each other's biggest supporters. No matter how busy they get, they always make time to hang out together, which is good because their lives are going to be more hectic than they ever could have imagined soon.

Demi's main focus over the next few years is to continue to pursue her music career. She just finished recording her debut album and is very proud of it. She can't wait for her fans to hear her songs and to get the chance to perform for them. After a summer spent on the road opening up for the Jonas Brothers, Demi's album will hit the shelves in the fall of 2008. She couldn't be more excited, and she's already looking forward to getting back in the studio and recording a second album! Demi wants to continue to develop her sound, write more songs, and find her own niche within the music world. She really looks up to artists who have had long careers and whose sounds have evolved over time to stay current. She never wants to disappoint her fans, and is dedicated to giving them a fresh, unexpected twist with every album she puts out. Demi would love to be headlining her own tour by the summer of 2009, because performing live is her favorite part of being a musician! Plus, she's learned a lot while on tour with the Jonas Brothers and she can't wait to design a show just for her fans.

But Demi isn't the only one who might be doing a little more rockin' out. Selena also has a great voice, and she is very interested in getting her own music career going. Demi's label, Hollywood Records, is also very interested in Selena. A source told E! Online that "Hollywood Records really wants Selena. Nothing's signed yet, but they're going after her in a strong way." Selena's cover of the Disney classic "Cruella De Vil" was a huge hit on Radio Disney, and Selena is really eager to get back into the studio, but she isn't looking for a solo career like Demi. "I'd like to do an album," she explained to *Variety*. Selena is definitely trying to stand apart with her music. She wants to record something with a little bit of fun, spunky attitude. As she told PBSKids.org, "I like rock/pop, I guess you could say. Sort of Avril Lavigne type of music. I've always said that I wanted to be in a band, so hopefully when I start my music I'll be in a band, not just solo. You know like, me and four guys, something that's different and cool. It's different from what any other Disney Channel star has done so far, and I like having people with me to lean on, and people to write with and have fun with." Selena's favorite band is Paramore, which is also made up of four guys and a female lead singer, so it's no wonder that that dynamic appeals to her. No matter who ends up in her band, Selena is sure to be a very fun performer to watch, with her energetic silliness and big voice.

Demi and Selena will also both continue to pursue acting. *Wizards of Waverly Place, Camp Rock*, and *Princess Protection Program* are all huge hits. Demi and Selena loved working together on *Princess Protection Program* and getting to do another film with each other would be a dream come true for the two girls. They would both also love it if Demi got to guest star on *Wizards of Waverly Place*. Demi and Selena always have a great time together, whether they are working or playing, but it's always more fun to have your BFF around when you are working. When it comes to the types of roles they are interested in, Demi and Selena are looking in different directions. Demi really enjoys doing movies, but she is ready for a new challenge and would love to book a role on a television series. Working on *As the Bell Rings* gave Demi a little taste of series work, and she's been itching for more ever since. She has already filmed a pilot for the Disney Channel called *Sketch Pad*. She's got her fingers crossed that it will get the green light and become a regular show, but if it doesn't, Demi will just keep trying. Disney really believes in Demi and Disney executives are dedicated to finding just the right role for this rockin' starlet. She'll keep auditioning for pilots until she finds the perfect show—so keep your eyes on the TV. Demi will definitely have her own series soon!

Demi might be focusing all of her energy on television, but Selena is searching for more film roles. She will continue to play Alex on *Wizards of Waverly Place* until the series ends, but the show doesn't film year-round. Selena has plenty of downtime to film other projects. *Princess Protection Program*, *Horton Hears a Who!*, and *Another Cinderella Story* were great starts, but Selena really wants to do more. She is looking for roles that really challenge her and test her acting chops. Selena is being very careful not to get locked in to a specific stereotype. She wants to have a long career filled with diverse film roles, and she knows that she needs to be picky about what she accepts now to achieve that. "Workwise, my role model is Rachel McAdams. I fell in love with her in the movie *Mean Girls*, I love how she spreads herself out. She did a teen movie, a romance, a comedy, a family movie, a thriller. She reinvents herself each time, and that's what I respect and love about her the most," Selena explained to PBSKids.org. Rachel McAdams is a great role model for Selena and hopefully Selena will have a chance to work with her idol in the future. When it comes to her next role, Selena already has something specific in mind. "I'd like to play a mean girl. I did play a mean girl on *Hannah Montana*, but I'd like to be the bad person in a movie. Just something different to challenge myself!" Selena told PBSKids.org. Selena made a great diva on *Hannah Montana*, so she's sure to be a hit as a mean girl!

Selena and Demi will also continue to take advantage of all of the cool promotional opportunities and special events that Disney comes up with for its stars. They both competed in the 2008 Disney Channel Games and gave fans a chance to see just how athletic they are. Both girls were strong competitors and they had a blast hanging out and competing in fun events like obstacle courses and dance-offs with their Disney friends. Demi was on the blue team, captained by Kiely Williams, and Selena was on the yellow team, captained by Kevin Jonas. The fanfare surrounding the games was especially fun for the girls. They got to ride in a special parade and there was even a superfun dance for all of the participants where they got to cut loose and get down together.

Selena has guest starred on several Disney shows and will probably do more of that—fans would definitely love to see her return as Mikayla on *Hannah Montana*. Demi became very close to Nick, Joe, and Kevin Jonas on the set of *Camp Rock* and on the road with them for their Burning Up tour, so there is a very good chance she'll make a guest appearance on their new show *J.O.N.A.S.* Both girls can also be seen out and about at Disney premieres, concerts, and events.

One thing is certain; both Demi and Selena will probably be working with Disney for a long time to come. Disney is like a second home to these two friends, and they are both very grateful to Disney executives for giving them a chance to do what they love every single day. Plus, neither Demi nor Selena is in any hurry to grow up. There will be plenty of time for more adult roles when they get older—for now they are both happy being kids!

CHAPTER 13
JUST HANGING OUT

When they aren't busy working, Demi and Selena love to hang out together and just be regular teenage girls. They don't get to see each other as much as they used to because they are usually working on different projects, traveling, or practicing, so any time they get to just sit and catch up is special to them. They love getting together for sleepovers, where they make Rice Krispie treats, watch their favorite movies, dance around to upbeat music, and talk about boys. Even these decidedly non-girly girls have their girly moments! Demi and Selena's friendship has lasted so long because both girls are so understanding of each other's lives. They have a ton in common, including acting, music, skateboarding, their taste in music and movies, and their love of being silly. But they also have separate interests, hobbies, and friends, and they don't need to spend every second together. They love it when they do get to see each other, but they are also okay when they don't—it just means they have more to talk about they do get to catch up!

Even when they aren't hanging out as much, Demi and Selena always have each other's backs. Selena is quick to tell anyone who will listen about her wonderful best friend, as she did to *Girls' Life Magazine.* "My best girl friend would be Demi Lovato, and she's from Texas as well. I actually met her when I did *Barney & Friends* when I was about 7. We both did that show together, and now we're 15 and we're still best friends. Now she's off working for [the] Disney Channel [the Jonas Brothers' *Camp Rock*]. It's almost weird. My best guy bud is Randy Hill, and he's still back in Texas, working at a skate shop. I can always go to him when I need someone to talk to." Demi and Randy both often turn to Selena for advice. Her down-to-earth, no-nonsense attitude makes her great at helping her friends. "He [Randy] always asks me about stuff. He's like, 'Well, I'm going on a date with this girl. Hey, can I wear this?' I laugh at him. I'm like, 'Yeah, you can wear that. It should be fine.' He'll ask me about what he should get a girl for a present and stuff like that," Selena explained to *Girls' Life Magazine.* Randy and

Demi are both always happy to return the favor and help Selena with anything she might need to talk about. Having best friends that they've known since childhood has been very important to both Selena and Demi. They knew each other before they were stars, so they keep each other down to earth and humble. Plus, they know each other so well that they can completely relax around each other and be as goofy as they want.

Although the girls are best friends and will always be there for each other, family comes first for both girls. Demi is very close to her sisters and mom. Demi and her big sister have been performing together since they were little and they are the best of friends. Dallas has always been one of Demi's biggest role models, and they talk on the phone all of the time when they are apart. Dallas is still making music and pursuing her singing and acting careers, and Demi supports her big sister as much as Dallas has always supported her. Luckily, even though both sisters work in entertainment, there isn't any sibling rivalry. They never go after the same parts and they always do their best to help each other whenever they can. Demi's little sister, Madison, often comes along to Demi's sets, so they've gotten more chances to bond lately. Madison even hit it off with Frankie Jonas, the Jonas Brothers' youngest brother, at a Disney party. So who knows, maybe Madison and Frankie will be starring on Disney Channel next! At the end of the day, Selena has one friend that trumps all of the others—her mom. "My mom is my best friend. She's always with me everywhere I go. Sometimes on set, I just need to see her face. I'm like, 'Mom, I need to see you.' I just have to have my mom," Selena explained to *Girls' Life Magazine*.

Selena is also very good friends with her *Wizards of Waverly Place* costars and they hang out almost as much off-set as they do on. "We text each other as soon as we leave set. We ask our parents, 'Can we go to the mall? Can we go to the movies?' I cried when the first season was over because my little brother [Jake T. Austin] was going back to New York, and my older brother [David Henrie] was going to Utah to shoot *Dadnapped*. So we call each other every day, 'What are you doing? I miss you,'" Selena told

Girls' Life Magazine. "I'm the only child so it's really cool to play the middle sister of two brothers on *Wizards*. It's cool to pretend I've known these people all my life and get in fights with them. It's really fun." Selena is so close with her costars, that there have been some rumors of Selena dating one of them. But Selena assured *Girls' Life Magazine* that she is, in fact, single. "No, actually I do not [have a boyfriend]. I don't. I'm traveling right now, and I'm only 15. I don't really think I necessarily need one now, and I'm not home. I'm not in California. I'm in Canada, so I'll be here for a while. So maybe around next year I'll have one then, but not right now. I'm focusing on work and school." There have also been rumors of Selena dating Cody Linley, who stars as Jake Ryan on *Hannah Montana.* But it was actually Demi who once dated the *Hannah* hottie. The two had taken acting classes together for quite a while, and one day they rehearsed a scene together and ended up talking for an hour afterward. They began dating after that and had a lot of fun together, but their conflicting schedules made it almost impossible for them to see each other very often. They eventually broke up, but they remain very close friends to this day.

One of the coolest things Selena does with her costars is surf. Selena, Jake T. Austin, and Jennifer Stone go surfing together every chance they get. "Jake recently did a movie where he surfed, and he told me I should try it. And I was like, 'Okay,' and I got really into it, it was so much fun. At first the ocean scared me a little bit, but we don't go too far out. Once you ride that first wave, there's something about it that keeps you riding more and more," Selena told PBSKids.org. Selena was quick to teach Demi to surf as well, and now it's a favorite activity for both girls. They see surfing as a way to let loose. It's just them and the water when they're riding the waves, and that's probably a really nice feeling for girls as busy as Selena and Demi. "My idea of getting away is going surfing. I go surfing in Malibu with Jake and Jen. I've surfed six hours in one day!" Selena explained to DiscoveryGirls.com. Selena and Demi also love to skateboard, but surfing is, by far, their favorite sport. "It's a stress relief. Like with surfing, it's nice to go on a beach and just forget about stuff and get away. It's fun. And acting's kind of like a sport for me too, it's the same as something like football or basketball for other people. It's something you do for fun and something you're serious about," Selena told PBSKids.org.

In addition to sporty activities like surfing and skateboarding, Demi's favorite thing to do when she has downtime is to work on her music. She loves playing guitar and piano and writing new songs. She and Dallas often have impromptu writing sessions together when they're both home. Demi also writes poetry and she loves playing around online. She tries to get in acting and dancing classes whenever she gets a chance so she can brush up on her basic skills and stay in shape for upcoming projects. But Demi spends most of her time off catching up with friends back in Texas and relaxing.

Considering how much Selena loves surfing, it makes sense that protecting the oceans and beaches is very important to her. Science has always been Selena's favorite subject, and she especially likes biology. "I have no idea why, but there's something about learning about our planet and everything else, even the specific things like learning about flowers or something. I really love it," Selena told *Girls' Life Magazine*. The more she learns about the delicate ecosystems in danger in her own home and around the world, the more Selena does to help out. Giving back to her community and using her popularity to increase awareness for causes that are important to her are high on Selena's list of priorities. "My family and I want to start our own organization to work on global warming and a couple of other things. It's kind of sad when you walk up to teens nowadays and you start talking about global warming, and half of them say, 'What?' I want to educate everyone about that situation . . . We just want to do as much as possible. We recycle; we do everyday little things that people don't think will matter. But in reality, those little things are the most important. Doing everything you can do and spreading the word," Selena told PBSKids.org. Hopefully all of Selena's efforts will inspire her friends and fans to pitch in for their favorite causes, too!

Demi is particularly devoted to a cause as well. She and her older sister have been performing in USO shows since they were little, going from military base to military base and putting on fantastic shows for the troops there. Demi is a firm believer in supporting the men and women who defend the United States, and she loves entertaining them. She will always be a big supporter of the USO and all that it does to make things better for the troops.

Selena and Demi may be ready to go out and save the world, but even they have to take a break sometimes! There are times when Selena and Demi get together, turn off their phones, fix their favorite snacks, and just veg out. They love watching movies, especially those starring their celebrity crushes. Selena loves Emile Hirsch and Shia LeBeouf. "My celebrity crush is, oh, what is his name? He was in *Alpha Dog* and *Into the Wild*. Emile Hirsch," Selena told *Girls' Life Magazine*. ". . . It was Shia LaBeouf, then I saw a couple of movies with Emile Hirsch, and I was like, 'I have a new crush.' He's so cute." It would probably be pretty cool for Selena to get the chance to be in a movie with Emile or Shia, and it could happen. Shia was a Disney Channel star himself when he was younger. He played Louis Stevens on the series *Even Stevens* and the lead role of Stanley Yelnats in the Disney feature film *Holes*. Demi's favorite actor is Jim Sturgess, who played the role of Jude in *Across the Universe*, the musical film written around the music of superstar band the Beatles. Demi has been a Beatles fan since she was little and she loved the film.

Even though neither of the girls have time to watch TV very often, Selena never misses her favorite show: *Gossip Girl*. "I'm not a huge TV person, but me and my mom every Wednesday night watch *Gossip Girl*. And we have all the shows that are on iTunes. *Gossip Girl*, I don't know why I love it. It's very well-acted. I admire everybody on that show," Selena explained to *Girls' Life Magazine*. Selena's favorite thing about the show? "Probably Blake Lively, the girl who plays Serena. I really admire her as an actress, and I hear she's a really sweet girl. I'd love to learn from her, how she takes direction and stuff like that. Plus, to meet her, that would be fun," Selena told *Girls' Life Magazine*.

Most people like to snack on popcorn or candy while watching movies and television, but not Selena and Demi.

Their favorite foods are a little more unconventional. "I love pickles. I have no idea why. I just love pickles. I guess I'm a sour girl," Selena told *Girls' Life Magazine*. In Texas, people can buy pickles in movie theaters, and that's one of the things that they miss most about Texas. When Selena made an appearance on *Ellen* in January 2008, Ellen DeGeneres could commiserate. Ellen lived in Texas once, too, and misses movie pickles just as much as Selena. She even gave Selena a pair of special Converse sneakers that she drew pickles on! Pickles are a little strange as a snack, but what's really weird is that Selena likes to eat lemons with salt. Demi prefers her lemons with sugar, but Selena has always gone for the salt shaker. "It actually started when I did *Barney*. At lunch, my friend Demi and a bunch of other castmates would put sugar on their lemons, but I didn't like it. It was too sweet. So I put salt on it, and I fell in love with it ever since," Selena told *Girls' Life Magazine*. The sour and salty combination really makes Selena happy and she eats lemons almost every day. "[Maria Canals-Barrera] who plays my mom on the show— she says, 'How can you eat a whole lemon?' She always says,

'It's because you're from Texas, that's why.' She always laughs at me, but I love lemons. I just have a whole lemon and put a little salt on it. My mom is getting on me for that because it's bad for my teeth. But I'm like, 'I brush every day, every night,' and she's like, 'It doesn't matter. It's going to get your enamel.' She's getting all mad at me," Selena told *Girls' Life Magazine.* Luckily for Selena's teeth, she stays away from foods with sugar and brushes and flosses regularly, so hopefully those lemons won't do too much damage! Selena's favorite drink to wash everything down is "Sugar-free Red Bull! I had a sip of my mom's and I was like, 'Oooh, this is good!' but she won't let me have too many. But every now and then, if I have a meeting or something, she'll let me. It gives me a little jolt of energy so I can focus on work or something!" she explained to *Popstar!*

Whether they are surfing, working for their favorite causes, or just goofing off together snacking and watching movies, Demi and Selena always have a great time. They may not have much time off these days, but they always make the most of it together!

CHAPTER 14
FASHION FORWARD

Selena and Demi may be best friends, but when it comes to their styles, these two girls have drastically different looks. Selena has a sporty chic vibe while Demi's clothes are a mix of her rocker persona and California cool. But one stylish thing they do have in common is a love of shopping. These two best friends really enjoy hitting up the mall and designer boutiques together in search of the perfect outfit, although Demi lasts a lot longer on those outings than Selena does! They both love Urban Outfitters, Forever 21, dELiA's, Hollister Co., Kitson, and Free People, but luckily they usually go for different pieces, so shopping together is always fun.

Selena achieves her flirty, casual style by pairing sporty pieces with more girly touches and accessories. She loves tube socks with fun stripes, ringer tees, hoodies, and funky shoes. Her favorites are Converse sneakers, as she explained to PBSKids.org. "I'm a huge Converse girl. I think I have about twenty pairs in different colors." Bright colors are a must for Selena, which is why she loves her colorful Converse so much. Neon hues and saturated jewel tones look great against Selena's olive skin and dark hair and she wears plenty of them. She also wears lots of skinny jeans and often pairs them with long, tunic-style tops. Selena loves the looks that were very popular in the 1980s—big, oversized, off-the-shoulder shirts with wide belts, leggings, ankle boots, and neon colors. She even has a bright yellow Member's Only jacket, which was one of the coolest brands to wear back in the eighties.

Selena definitely likes to look cute, but it's more important to her that her outfits are fun and easy to move around in—just in case she wants to play a pickup basketball game or chase her television brothers around the set. "I can't dress in something that I'm not comfortable in," Selena told PBSKids.org. But even sporty Selena can't always avoid dressing up. She has to amp up her style when its time to hit the red carpet or attend an event. "I do understand that I can't wear jeans and sneakers to an event, but I'm not a dress girl. I can't do dresses or extreme high heels. So I find my own way of dressing up! I like to add cool bracelets or skinny jeans. I try to find a happy medium," Selena told PBSKids.org. Selena is really into funky jewelry and she owns tons of necklaces, bracelets, and big earrings. Plus she has plenty of cool fringed boots, printed heels, and brightly colored and metallic sandals. Shoes can really make or break an outfit, and Selena has plenty of shoes to choose from—her collection would make any girl jealous! But at the end of the day, it's not about what she wears, it's more about how she wears it. "Self-confidence is a huge part of it. You can't think that you're not as good as anyone else. And I think it's important to be careful of what you do and say and who you hang out with. Represent yourself well, even in the clothes you wear," Selena explained to PBSKids.org.

Confidence is key, but it never hurts to put the finishing touches on a look! Selena likes to look polished, but not overdone. She wears very light makeup—usually just a dusting of bronzer, blush, a few coats of black mascara, and clear lip gloss. However, for a glamorous event Selena will add some darker lipstick or gloss and some smoky eye shadow. Most of the time Selena wears her long, shiny black hair down, either straightened or curled into soft, loose waves. But when she's playing sports, she'll put it in a ponytail, and for events, she's been known to pin it up so that she can pretend to have shorter hair for an evening.

Selena's look is fun, fresh, and easygoing, so it's no wonder that the stylists on *Wizards of Waverly Place* modeled her character's style after hers. Alex is just as spunky and sporty as Selena is. She wears lots of bright colors, layers, tube socks, and, of course, fun sneakers. "I wear the Converse and Vans and funky tops and chunky jewelry, but I don't get in trouble as much as she [Alex] does!" Selena explained to *Teen* magazine. One of the coolest things about having the same sense of style as her character is that it's like having an amazing second wardrobe. Selena loves getting dressed for filming every day, especially since she occasionally gets to keep some of the clothes! Selena even gets a say in Alex's wardrobe from time to time. "Wardrobe would always talk to me and get ideas from the clothes I'd wear to the set. Now my character wears nothing but Converse! That's so fun for me because I get to wear different Converse all the time," Selena told DiscoveryGirls.com. As the show has gone on, Selena has gotten the opportunity to wear funkier, funnier, and more interesting costumes. In the episode where she and Justin go to Wiz Tech, Selena had to wear a long, dark robe and round, plastic glasses. She probably felt pretty goofy in that *Harry Potter* style getup, but she looked great as usual. Jake, who plays Selena's younger brother on the show, got to dress up like a sub sandwich in one episode and David, who plays her older brother, got to get funky wearing a zebra sport coat for a prom episode—so who knows what Selena will get to wear next!

Demi isn't quite as sporty as her best friend, so it's no surprise that Demi's look is pretty different from Selena's. Demi lives and breathes rock and roll, so her outfits can be a little edgy. Black and red are two of her favorite colors, and she's often seen sporting an all-black ensemble with just a pop of red—like a bright red clutch bag or a pair of red ankle boots. Demi loves turtlenecks, black jeans, and hats of all kinds. She owns fedoras, berets, skullcaps, newsboy hats, and even a baseball cap or two! Demi's typical rock-star outfit consists of skinny, dark-wash jeans, a black top, and a funky fedora, with a big necklace, high heels, and bright red lipstick. That way she's always ready to step into the spotlight.

When Demi isn't up on stage performing, she's just a typical laid-back Texas girl. She loves sundresses, especially peasant style in dusty colors and busy patterns, which she usually pairs with wide belts that accentuate her waist. She also loves to add brightly colored pumps and big, eye-catching jewelry. When she's just hanging out with her friends, skateboarding with Selena, or working in the studio, Demi goes for a casual, comfy vibe. She likes brightly colored skinny jeans, cozy sweaters, hooded sweatshirts with girly details like ruffles and ribbons, and T-shirts with funny or inspirational sayings on them. Like Selena, Demi has a soft spot for 1980s style and can often be found rocking suspenders, neon prints, and legwarmers.

One of Demi's favorite ways to make her look stand

out is to play with makeup. She keeps her look simple during the day with lip gloss, a little blush, and mascara, but when she's ready to hit the stage, Demi goes all out. She loves lipsticks in red or maroon, jewel-toned eye shadow, and a little bit of black eyeliner. Slightly heavier makeup is easier to see from the audience, and Demi always wants to make sure her fans can see her when she's singing for them. Even when she rocks wild makeup, Demi keeps her hair pretty basic. She has gorgeous, long, shiny, dark-brown hair with adorable bangs, and she usually wears it down and straight. She does pull her bangs back from time to time, put her hair halfway up, or even into a 1980s style side ponytail. Experimenting with different hairstyles is especially fun for events or concerts. But when Demi is relaxing or hanging out with friends, she likes to keep her look low-key and chill. Of course, Demi's favorite hairstyles almost always involve a cool and funky hat that helps her stand out in a crowd!

Dressing up like your favorite stars can be really fun, but to get either Selena or Demi's looks, the best thing you can do is be confident and feel good about yourself. Both of these stars have a lot of fun with their style and never care whether anyone else likes what they are wearing—it's all about wearing what makes them feel best!

CHAPTER 15
BFF PLAYLIST

Selena and Demi certainly know how to rock out. But these two BFFs love listening to music almost as much as they like performing it. Music is one of the most important things in both of their lives and they are seriously passionate about their favorite bands. Luckily, both girls like a lot of the same singers and groups, which makes it easy to choose what to listen to when they are hanging out! These are just a few of their favorites, but Selena and Demi are always on the lookout for great new acts, so they are sure to have some new favorites to add to their MP3 players soon.

PARAMORE—Paramore is a pop-rock band with a gritty edge from Franklin, Tennessee, made up of Zac Farro, Jeremy Davis, Josh Farro, and rockin' female lead singer Hayley Williams. Paramore hit it big with their single "Misery Business" in the summer of 2007 and scored major airtime on MTV. Both Demi and Selena claim Paramore as their all-time favorite band. They love Hayley's edgy style and aggressive delivery. She's a strong woman, and she and her band work hard to inspire musical girls everywhere to let loose and rock.

BRITNEY SPEARS—Britney Spears is an American pop star who rose to fame when she was only fifteen years old. She has sold over eighty-three million records worldwide and won numerous awards. Britney has gone through some rough times, and has most recently been known more for the controversy surrounding her than for her music. Britney started her career on the Disney Channel show *The New Mickey Mouse Club.* Selena has loved Britney since she was little. "I've been to every single one of Britney Spears's concerts. Yeah, I have faith in Britney. I love her to death, and of course, everyone goes through rough patches," Selena told *Girls' Life Magazine.*

KELLY CLARKSON—Kelly Clarkson is a superstar singer and has really inspired Demi. This sassy Texas beauty won the first season of the hit talent competition *American Idol* and has been inspiring girls everywhere ever since. From powerful ballads to catchy girl-power anthems, Kelly's music is always in demand. Her fun songs cover breakups, romance, and friendship, and they are great for Selena and Demi to sing along to on road trips and at karaoke.

THE JONAS BROTHERS—The Jonas Brothers are a brother act from New Jersey and are good friends of Demi and Selena. Nick, Joe, and Kevin Jonas became famous thanks to their infectious blend of pop, punk, and rock and roll, and their adorable good looks. These supercute boys have released two albums, sold out tour dates, and are starring in *Camp Rock* with Demi! Their music is fun and easy to listen to and it always puts Selena and Demi in a good mood.

VALENCIA—Valencia is a punk-rock band from Philadelphia, Pennsylvania, made up of Shane Henderson, JD Perry, Maxim Soria, George Ciukurescu, and Brendan

Walter. They have toured with another Demi-and-Selena favorite, Boys Like Girls. They have a fun, up-tempo sound—even when they are singing about sad topics. Their music can probably always cheer Demi and Selena up, no matter how bad a day they've had.

THE POSTAL SERVICE—The Postal Service is an electronic indie-pop act that began as a collaboration on one song between Ben Gibbard of Death Cab for Cutie and James Tamborello of Dntel, Headset, and Figurine. The two were so inspired by the collaboration that they decided to release an entire album in 2003. They had high-profile guest performers on many of their songs and fans of their other bands loved the album. They have yet to release a second album, but no one has ruled it out yet, since they have been brainstorming ideas for years. Their music is generally mellow and is great to listen to at the end of a long, hard day.

JOAN JETT—Joan Jett is a true revolutionary. She was one of the founding members of the girl group the Runaways from the 1970s. She went solo toward the end of the 1970s and is most well known for her 1982 hit "I Love Rock and Roll." Joan inspired girls everywhere to chop off their hair, throw on a leather jacket, and show the boys that girls could rock, too. She has played the guitar, written songs, sang, produced, and been an actress over the course of her career, and has remained relevant in the music business for almost forty years. Demi and Selena really look up to Joan and they are both hoping their careers will be as long and successful as hers.

THE ALMOST—The Almost is a drum-heavy rock band from Ocala, Florida, made up of Aaron Gillespie, Dusty Redmon, Jay Vilardi, Alex Aponte, and Kenny Bozich. Aaron Gillespie, who is also the drummer for the band Underoath, was inspired by the Foo Fighters to start the Almost as a way to step into the spotlight and showcase a more melodic side of his musical ability. Dancing and jumping around to the Almost's rhythmic beats is a great way for Demi and Selena to get out excess energy.

FOREVER THE SICKEST KIDS—Forever the Sickest Kids is an electronic-fused power pop band from Dallas, Texas. Austin Bello, Kyle Burns, Jonathan Cook, Kent Garrison, Marc Stewart, and Caleb Turman joined up in 2006 and they've been on a roll ever since. They participated in the popular Warped Tour in 2007 and their energetic stage show really drew in fans. Demi and Selena love their infectious sound and their music is perfect to listen to before a big day of surfing or a game of basketball.

DAPHNE LOVES DERBY—Daphne Loves Derby is a mellow alternative act made up of Stu Clay, Kenny Choi, Spencer Abbott, and David Sparks. They got their unique name when they were playing a big music festival and another band had the same name they did. Kenny shouted out the name "Daphne Loves Derby" just for that show, but everyone liked it so much that it stuck! Their low-key brand of independent pop music is great for Demi and Selena to listen to when they need to unwind in their trailers while filming, or when they just need a break to relax.

LANDON PIGG—Landon Pigg is a bluesy singer-songwriter based out of Nashville, Tennessee. His smooth vocals, simple but poignant lyrics, and sweet melodies are making his fans everywhere swoon. Demi and Selena definitely appreciate Landon's willingness to wear his heart on his sleeve in his music. It's easy to relate to his songs because of their honest, straightforward emotional appeal.

MAZZY STAR—Mazzy Star is a dreamy pop band that was popular in the early 1990s. It was made up of guitarist David Roback and bassist Kendra Smith, who was later replaced by Hope Sandoval. Mazzy Star's sound is a throwback to the psychedelic pop bands of the 1960s and 1970s. Their biggest hit, "Fade Into You," was very popular when Demi and Selena were toddlers, so listening to this duo probably brings back happy childhood memories.

FAREWELL—Farewell is pop-punk band from Greensboro, North Carolina. These charming southern boys really know how to rock out. Marshall Davis, Wil Andrews, Kevin Carter, Buddy Bell, Jeff Ellis, and Chris Lee make up Farewell. They've been influenced by popular bands like Blink 182 and Fall Out Boy, and their energetic songs are just plain fun to listen to. Selena and Demi must enjoy putting Farewell on and dancing around their rooms.

ACCEPTANCE—Acceptance was a rocking emo band from Seattle, Washington, made up of Jason Vena, Nick Radovanovic, Ryan Zwiefelhofer, Kaylan Cloyd, and Christian McAlhaney. These adorable boys are most well known for their catchy, but deeply emotional songs, and many of their fans claim that Acceptance's music has helped them through some pretty hard times. It's definitely good music for Demi and Selena to listen to when they are feeling down in the dumps.

MISSY HIGGINS—Missy Higgins is an Australian singer-songwriter with a mellow, independent vibe and a heavily acoustic sound. Her lyrics are poignant and heartfelt, and her deep, soulful voice inspires her fans. Her debut album topped the charts in Australia and went platinum nine times. Missy's songs are perfect for Demi and Selena to throw on when they've had a long stressful day or are having boy problems.

FOUR YEAR STRONG—Four Year Strong is a hardcore rock-and-roll band from Massachusetts. Most of the members met in high school, and the band is well known for laying pop style vocals over a rock-and-roll melody with sporadic bursts of screaming, gang vocals, and double bass. It is made up of Dan O'Connor, Alan Day, Joe Weiss, Jackson "Jake" Massucco, and Josh Lyford. These scruffy rocker boys always put on a great show and their high-energy albums are the perfect soundtrack when Demi and Selena go skateboarding or just need to pump themselves up before a big scene.

CHAPTER 16
FUN, FAST BEST FRIEND FACTS
SELENA GOMEZ

FULL NAME: Selena Kayleigh Gomez

NICKNAME: Sel

BIRTH DATE: July 22, 1992

BIRTHPLACE: New York, New York

HOMETOWN: Grand Prairie, Texas

HEIGHT: 5' 5"

HAIR COLOR: Dark brown

EYE COLOR: Brown

PARENTS: Mandy Teefy and stepdad Brian

SIBLINGS: None

STAR SIGN: Cancer

CELEB CRUSH: Shia LaBeouf

FAVORITE THANKSGIVING FOOD: Stuffing

FAVORITE PIZZA TOPPINGS: Cheese, mushrooms, jalapeños

FAVORITE SUBJECT: Science

FAVORITE FRUIT: Mangoes

FAVORITE MOVIE: *Alice in Wonderland* and *The Wizard of Oz*

FAVORITE ACTRESS: Rachel McAdams

HOBBIES: Cheerleading, singing, surfing, skateboarding

FAVORITE BAND: Paramore

PETS: Four dogs, including Chip, a mutt Selena rescued from her local animal shelter

DEMI LOVATO

FULL NAME: Demetria Devonne Lovato

NICKNAME: Demi

BIRTH DATE: August 20, 1992

BIRTHPLACE: Dallas, Texas

HEIGHT: 5' 2"

HAIR COLOR: Brown

EYE COLOR: Brown

PARENTS: Dianna Lovato

SIBLINGS: Older sister Dallas Lovato and younger sister Madison Lovato

STAR SIGN: Leo

CELEB CRUSH: William Beckett from the band The Academy Is and Jim Sturgess

INSTRUMENTS: Guitar and piano

FAVORITE MOVIE: *Donnie Darko*

FAVORITE CELEBRITY: Kelly Clarkson

FAVORITE CLOTHING: Hats

FAVORITE FOODS: Pickles, cheese, eggs, Rice Krispie treats, chocolate

FAVORITE COLORS: Red and black

FAVORITE FRUIT: Oranges

HOBBIES: Surfing, basketball, writing songs

FAVORITE BAND: Paramore

PET PEEVE: Rumors

BFF FACTS

FAVORITE SNACK TO MAKE TOGETHER: Rice Krispie treats

FRIENDSHIP JEWELRY: Matching pink guitar pick necklaces

SECRET HANDSHAKE: A clapping combination to the Kit Kat candy jingle

WHERE THEY MET: At the audition for *Barney & Friends*

FAVORITE THINGS TO DO TOGETHER: Shop, surf, and make videos

CHAPTER 17
THE GIRLS ONLINE

Demi and Selena are seriously busy best friends! Whether they are filming television shows or movies, auditioning, working in the recording studio, or just hanging out with each other, there's no telling where they'll be next or what they'll be doing. So if you want to keep up with these talented starlets, here is a list of websites with all of the latest Selena and Demi information.

You can do a lot of cool stuff on the Internet, like play games, chat with friends, or watch hilarious YouTube videos like the ones that Demi and Selena make together, but they would always want you to be careful when you are hanging out online. Never give out any sort of personal information—like your name, address, phone number, or the name of your school or sports team—and never try to meet someone in person that you met online. And never surf the web without your parents' permission.

When you are online, please remember that not

everything you read there is true. There are lots of people creating websites, and sometimes they make up information to make their sites more exciting. And don't worry if your favorite websites disappear. Websites come and go, so don't worry—there's sure to be more Selena and Demi sites to replace them soon!

www.youtube.com/user/therealdemilovato

This is Selena and Demi's official YouTube channel. They created this page so that they could communicate directly with their fans as best friends. Check it out to see all of their hilarious videos!

www.myspace.com/demilovato

This is Demi Lovato's official MySpace page. It has all of the updates on her music, movies, and television appearances.

www.myspace.com/selenagomez

This is Selena Gomez's official MySpace page.

www.tv.disney.go.com/disneychannel/ wizardsofwaverlyplace/index.html

This is the official *Wizards of Waverly Place* Disney Channel site and it has tons of fun activities, extras, and information about Selena and the rest of the cast.

www.selenagomezfan.com

This is a great Selena fan site with a biography, pictures, and all of the latest Selena news.

www.demi-lovato.com

This is a rockin' Demi fan site with fun facts, music updates, and pictures.